This book is presented to:

Cecil B. Moore

From:

On this day:

Message:

Professor, May I Bring My Baby to Class?

**A Student-Mother's Guide to College
with Journal and Real-Life Success Stories**

Sherrill W. Mosee

FCS Books
Philadelphia, PA

The child care checklist reprinted by permission of NACCRRA, © 2008, http://www.naccrra.org, "Is This the Right Place for My Child? 38 Research-Based Indicators of High-Quality Child Care."

FCS Books
8001 Castor Avenue, #501
Philadelphia, PA 19152
Tel: (877) 264-9915
www.fcsbooks.com

Ordering Information

Quantity sales. Special discounts are available on quantity purchases by educational institutions, organizations, corporations, and others. For details, contact the "Special Sales Department" at the FCS Books address above.

Individual sales. FCS Books publications are available through most bookstores. They can also be ordered directly from FCS Books at (877) 264-9915.

Orders by U.S. trade bookstores and wholesalers. Please contact Cardinal Publishers Group: Tel: (800) 296-0481; Fax: (317) 879-0872, www.cardinalpub.com.

Family Care Solutions, Inc., is a registered trademark, www.familycaresolutions.org.
Printed in the United States of America

Publisher's Cataloging-in-Publication data

Mosee, Sherrill W.
    Professor, may I bring my baby to class? A student mother's guide to college
with journal and real-life success stories / Sherrill W. Mosee.
        p. cm.
        Includes index and bibliographical references.
        ISBN 978-0-9642843-9-5
1. Teenage mothers—United States—Life skills guides. 2. Teenage mothers—Education (Higher)—United States. 3. Single mothers—United States—Life skills guides. 4. Single mothers—Education (Higher)—United States. 5. Motherhood—United States. I. Title.

HQ759.4 .M665 2009
306.874322-dc22   2009905882

First Edition
14 13 12 11 10 09   10 9 8 7 6 5 4 3 2 1

Cover design and interior composition: Fuiano Design
Copyediting: PeopleSpeak

Contents

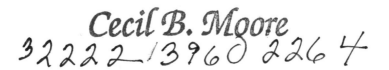

Chapter 3   **What Can I Do about Child Care?**   **65**

Chapter 4   **How to Become a Successful Student-Parent**   **93**

Preface

My mother was excited when she got her acceptance letter to attend Penn State University in 1959. She had worked so hard to maintain her grades after giving birth to my older brother two years earlier at age sixteen. It wasn't easy back then, nor is it today, to care for a baby and go to school, but my mother knew that furthering her education would help provide a good life for her and her son. She didn't know how she was going to manage school and a child. She would figure it out later.

When she shared the news with her mother, my grandmother, her excitement turned to sorrow as her dream of going to college was ripped away in a moment. My grandmother looked at my brother and told my mother that her college degree was standing in front of her. Because of him, college was not an option; she had to get a job.

Even today, fifty years later, our dreams can be taken away from us by the very people we depend on to encourage us. My grandmother's reaction is still shared today by many people who believe that a young mother has ruined her life and lost all her opportunities for a brighter future. Telling someone she can't do something snips her wings, limits her ability to fly, and restricts her potential.

My mother married later that year. I came along a few years later, followed by another brother and a sister. My parents separated when I was five and later divorced. Growing up in Baltimore, Maryland, I watched my mom struggle to provide the basics for her children—housing, food, and clothing. I don't remember going to the doctor's regularly. I only saw the dentist when he visited my school for cavity-prevention week. My mom would always tell us that we could be and could do anything we wanted to as long as we believed we could. I believed I was going to become the first African-American female astronaut, so I decided to major in aeronautical engineering. She never said, "Are you crazy? You can't do that!" Neither one of us really knew what aeronautical engineering was. As usual, she encouraged me and believed in whatever I believed in. With my mother on my side, I always felt strong, confident, and powerful.

I consider three events in my adult life to be difficult times: giving birth to my children, going to college to study engineering, and writing this book. But as with doing the first two, I knew I had to write it. My journey began when I moved to Philadelphia in 1986, married, and became a first-time mom a few years later. When I couldn't find resources to help identify neighborhood child care providers, I decided to create a child care directory to help working parents like myself. Little did I know the directory would later serve another purpose. In 1996, my stepdaughter became pregnant during her first year of college at Lincoln University in Pennsylvania. She had family support to help care for her baby. I wondered what happened to the many young mothers who didn't have support or couldn't afford child care, college tuition, and household expenses. My assumption was they would drop out of school.

Very little information about student-parents in college was available at that time. Pennsylvania didn't offer much financial help either. In 1998, I formed a nonprofit organization, Family Care Solutions, Inc., and created a child care scholarship to help low-income single mothers pay for child care so they could continue their education. Child care providers listed in the directory became sponsors to help support the college moms. Helping student-parents with child care assistance is now my full-time job. I absolutely love what I do. I've helped hundreds of women, and a few men, over the years. I've had the privilege of getting to know the student-parents I serve. I hear their stories of how they've persevered with and without support. I am always amazed by their courage and their will to push past their obstacles to succeed.

As I began speaking to teen moms and other groups of women not enrolled in college, I realized that this population wasn't getting the message: you can go to college with a baby. My prayer is that this book will reach the one who doesn't believe college is possible, the one whose dream was crushed when she was told she couldn't go to college with a baby, the one who is experiencing hard times and doesn't see college in her future, or the one who feels like giving up.

∾

Acknowledgments

I am blessed that God chose me to write this book. It has been a humbling and rewarding experience. I am deeply indebted to all those who took part in shaping this book. Thank you to the thirty-one beautiful and courageous women who opened their hearts to share their stories with the world: Rita Anusionwu, Michelle Artibee, Talia Barrows, Deneisha Cauthen, Anna Connors, Jessica Coombe, De'Asia Davis, Dawn Gallagher-Gonzalez, NaTasha Goodman, Roslinda Harris, LaKeesha Holloman, Kameela Howard, Jessica Jamora, Tiffany Jenkins-Stevens, Kassandra Kuehl, Desiree LaMarr, La-Kee-a Lowry, Melissa Mendez-Arechiga, Ayesha Mosee, Kendra Newman, Moneek Pines-Elliott, Rasheedah Phillips, Rebecca Precht, Danielle Raitt, Tammy Richardson, Sara Rulle, Lautauscha Shell, Sandra Simon, Annette Sokolnicki, Catella Visser, and Beverly Wiginton. Your inspirational stories about the struggles and triumphs of going to college with a child make this book come alive.

Thank you to my wonderful husband, George, for allowing me to spread my wings and dream as big as I want to and for always being available to help; to my beautiful children, Darius and Asia, for encouraging me and enduring my late nights and many requests to read portions of this book; to my sister, Jackie Parker, for cheering me on and writing my first "review" as she envisioned it would appear in the media.

Thank you to my close friend and college roommate, Teresa Holmes, for being brutally honest with your comments, and to my good friends, Bethea Eichwald and Adrienne Walls, for your many years of support and encouragement through the highs and lows. Thank you to my dear friends Naiema Vicks and Dahvry Henderson for your sweet spirits and for always being available to provide any

assistance needed, especially through the rough times. Thanks to
Katherine Truitt and Ellen Torrance for taking on the research project
and providing additional administrative support. Thank you to
Michelle Sewell who shared her experiences of becoming a published
author and to Jennifer Stein for providing guidance and sharing her
wisdom in the elements of publishing a book from start to finish.
Thank you to Sharon Goldinger and her team for doing a meticulous
job in editing the manuscript. You make me look good. Thank you
to Lou Fuiano, who took my breath away when I first saw the cover
design. You are incredibly talented.

Thank you to student-parents Rachel DeStefanis and Deahna
Byrd for sharing tips on how to prepare for the first day of classes
and to Dr. Rosetta Stith for opening the doors at the Laurence G.
Paquin Middle/Secondary School for Expecting and Parenting Teens
in Baltimore, Maryland, and to her students for reviewing selected
stories. Thank you to Adrienne McKinney for sharing important tips
about considering a child care provider.

A special thank you to the review committee for their invaluable
input and expert advice on the book's content and structure: Ann
Schmieg, Colleen McCauley, Lola Rooney, Cheryl Browning, Angela
Kweon, Candace Powell Kinard, Kathy Fisher, Dr. Karen Wells, Abby
Binder, Elizabeth Lower-Basch, Marlene Weinstein, Alba Martinez,
and Dr. Mary Sciaraffa and student-parents Tina Marie Keoseyan and
Kirston Ransom. It was their insight and professional experiences
that helped refine the book's message.

Thank you to State Senator Shirley M. Kitchen for helping me
secure funding to support student-parents in college and to Dr.
Joseph Williams for taking the pressure off and allowing me to focus
on my work. Thank you to Doria Mitchell for lending your heart and
passion to the work of the organization. Thanks also to my wonderful
board of directors for catching the vision and providing support:
Rendell Bradley, Tifani Cottingham, Michael Krautkramer, Curtis

Jenkins, Jennifer Halliday, and Rasheedah Phillips. Thank you to the Connelly Foundation and Claneil Foundation for funding this project.

And most importantly, thank you to my mom, Ella Tate, who passed away during the writing of this book. Thank you for giving me your heart, soul, and spirit. Thank you for always believing in my dreams. I will never forget you saying, "If you can dream it, you can do it." ∾

Introduction

Professor, May I Bring My Baby to Class? is a guide that offers inspiration through short stories written by college moms across the country along with tips and resources to help you on your journey in pursuit of a college degree. You'll find information about colleges and universities that offer on-campus child care, housing for women and children, financial aid, and other support services for student-parents. It's also a journal to allow you to tell your own story.

How to Get the Most from Your Journal

Use the journal pages as a place to write your story. Share your challenges and triumphs, dreams and aspirations. Answer the questions, complete the exercises, attach pictures of your children, yourself, and family members. Use the blank pages to journal, take notes, and write about milestones. It will be fun going back, years from now, to read about your experiences while going to school with a child (or children).

Each chapter includes short stories, a journal section, and facts related to the subject discussed.

Meet the Mother These women share their experiences of going to college with a child in hopes of encouraging you to pursue higher education.

Keeping It Real Here you can write down your personal thoughts about the subject discussed in that section.

Did You Know? These sidebars contain facts to make you more informed about the subject discussed.

The following tables, charts, and journal sections are included in the book:

Resources Here you'll find helpful Web sites and resources for financial aid, scholarships, and grants as well as organizations, educational programs, and social service agencies that can provide support and information to you.

Student-Parent Support Programs This table lists colleges and universities that offer on-campus child care, housing for students and their children, financial assistance, and other services to help you.

Is This the Right Place for My Child? Use this chart as a checklist to help you identify and choose quality child care.

Managing My Schedule Use these pages to keep up with your daily activities—classes, finals, doctor appointments, work, and so on.

As you read, it may be helpful to keep in mind these comments about the use of words:

▶ I use the words "school" and "college" interchangeably. They are both used when referring to all postsecondary institutions— colleges, universities, and career schools.

▶ Even though my writing usually refers to one child, please know that the information applies to you no matter how many children you have.

▶ It's cumbersome to use the phrase "he or she," so I try to alternate using he and she in my writing. Again, please know that the information applies to you, whether your child is male or female.

▶ I will often ask you to refer to your state's Web site for additional information. Please know that I am also including those of you who live in our nation's capital, the District of Columbia.

It is my hope that this book will encourage you to pursue your life's dreams through education. When graduation day approaches, you can proudly add this book to your collection of textbooks. However, this will be one book you will not want to resell. I hope it will become a keepsake and serve as a reminder that nothing is impossible, a valuable attribute you can pass on to your children.

Visit us on the Web at http://www.studentparentjournal.com. You can network with other student-parents and graduates, and find great information about more programs, services, and resources. ❧

CHAPTER 1

Can I Really Go to College with a Baby?

Your decision to go to college starts with the Power of You. You are beautiful. You are strong. You are brave. You are resilient. You are bold. You are kind. You are valuable. You are intelligent. You are loved. What you need to succeed is already in you. It's called your will. So, dig deep to pull Ms. Will out of her hiding place. Believe that you can graduate from high school, take care of your child, go to college, and graduate.

Begin to dream and visualize where you want to be three years from now and ten years from now. You can be whatever you dream of being. Never mind what others may say or do to discourage you. Hold your head up high. It's the only way you can see where you are going—toward your future.

Never limit yourself because of others' limited imagination; never limit others because of your own limited imagination.

Mae Jemison

What are my dreams?

_____

_____

_____

_____

Keeping it **REAL**

DREAMS (continued)

Keeping it REAL

_____

_____

_____

_____

_____

_____

_____

_____

_____

_____

_____

_____

_____

_____

_____

_____

_____

That was easy, right?

_____

_____

_____

Professor, May I Bring My Baby to Class?

WHY IS IT IMPORTANT FOR ME TO GO TO COLLEGE?

A college degree will change the way you live. If you are the first in your family to go to college, your decision could impact your family for generations. How? If you go to college, it is likely that your children will go too.

Higher education can break the cycle of poverty in your family. When you earn a college degree, you can make more money to better take care of your family and enjoy life. More opportunities will become available to you. You are not limited to live in certain neighborhoods or confined to work at certain jobs. Your quality of life will improve.

It doesn't matter if you live in a single-parent household, a two-parent household, foster care, a group home, or a shelter. When you pursue higher education, you will begin to value the importance of education and will undoubtedly pass those values on to your children. Children who see their mothers working hard to study and care for them while going to school will learn that they too must work hard to make their dreams come true. As they grow older, your children will begin to appreciate your commitment and will adopt your work ethic. As your children's first teacher, you become their role model and hero, instead of some famous athlete or celebrity they have never met.

How will a college education change my life?

_____

_____

_____

_____

Keeping it REAL

CHANGE MY LIFE (continued)

_____

_____

_____

_____

_____

_____

_____

_____

_____

_____

_____

_____

_____

_____

_____

_____

_____

_____

_____

_____

_____

_____

_____

Keeping it REAL

Professor, May I Bring My Baby to Class?

How do I hope my choice to go to college will affect my children's lives?

_____

_____

_____

_____

_____

_____

_____

_____

_____

_____

_____

_____

Glue a picture of your child here.

_____

_____

_____

_____

_____

_____

Your Estimated Annual Salary

Going to college and getting your degree can make a huge difference in your earning potential. A person with a high school diploma working as an entry-level retail cashier can earn a salary ranging from $16,901 to $23,093 a year depending on where she lives.[1] Is this enough to run a household and take care of your children?

What would you like to earn?

I'd like to earn an annual salary of _____.

Let's see if your desired salary is enough to take care of your personal, household, and child care expenses. Using the chart on the next page, estimate your monthly household bills or what you expect to pay when you are on your own. When you're done, multiply the total by twelve for your estimated annual salary.

DID YOU KNOW?

Most people's earning potential is measured by their education. Getting a degree, certificate, or professional degree is key to earning higher wages. The mean annual earnings for 2007 based on the level of education were as follows:

Less than a high school diploma: $21,251

A high school diploma or GED: $31,286

Some college experience, but no degree: $33,009

An associate degree: $39,746

A bachelor's degree: $57,181

A master's degree: $70,186

A doctorate degree: $95,565

A professional degree: $120,978[2]

Salaries vary depending on where you live, your profession, and your work experience. Traditionally, women earn less than men regardless of their level of education. Fortunately, on January 29, 2009, President Barack Obama signed his first bill into law, the Lilly Ledbetter Fair Pay Act, calling for equal pay for equal work for all.[3]

Professor, May I Bring My Baby to Class?

HOUSEHOLD BUDGET

Estimated Monthly Expenses

Mortgage/rent	
Child care	
Food	
Baby needs	
Clothes	
Homeowner's or renter's insurance	
Family health insurance	
Gas	
Electricity	
Water	
Phone	
Cell phone	
Car payment	
Car insurance	
Gas for car	
Public transportation	
School tuition/loan	
Credit cards	
Savings	
Emergency fund	
Entertainment	
Other:	
Other:	
Other:	
Total	
x 12 months = annual salary	

Does the total surprise you? Check the annual earnings in the "Did You Know" box on the previous page, and you'll see that you will need some form of higher education to earn what you've determined is needed to care for your family.

7

OVERCOMING YOUR OBSTACLES

Imagine breaking down society's stereotype of you as someone who is destined to fail. Now, imagine changing your destiny. It starts with trusting and believing in yourself to overcome your obstacles and is followed by taking action to change your situation. Thousands of young women just like you have found their strength and persevered through adversity to go to college and graduate. Some experienced domestic abuse, homelessness, drug addiction, rape, imprisonment, or depression. Some are women you see every day—bankers, teachers, social workers, and nurses. Some are doctors, engineers, lawyers, corporate executives, and computer analysts. These women are like you—women with children, women who exercised their power to change their destinies.

Your success starts with your healing and your triumph over the fears and perceptions that are preventing you from taking action. Believe that you have the potential to do great things. Your future contributions could help find a cure for cancer, develop break-through technologies, improve the public school system, or end world hunger. If you are experiencing difficult times and your situation seems like more than you can handle alone, seek professional assistance from organizations and agencies in your community. Begin by calling your local department of human services, department of social services, places of worship, or public housing agency. See appendix A for suggested organizations and Web sites that can help you address the many different needs you may have.

What are my obstacles?

_____

_____

_____

Keeping it REAL

Professor, May I Bring My Baby to Class?

OBSTACLES (continued)

_____

_____

_____

_____

_____

_____

_____

How will I begin to address my obstacles?

_____

_____

_____

_____

_____

_____

_____

_____

_____

_____

_____

Keeping it REAL

DON'T LISTEN TO THE "HATERS"

Are you excited about going to college? Nervous too? It's okay. Remember, you are on your way to building a brighter future for your family. Higher education symbolizes change to a better life and opens doors to new possibilities. Of course, with a child you are sure to face big challenges as you continue your journey through school. Some challenges you will face are not circumstances but people. Now that you have a baby, some people will tell you that you can't go to college. These are the "haters." They will give you all the reasons why you can't go: you have a baby, you don't have a high school diploma, you don't have money to go to school, you don't have anyone to watch your baby, you don't have money to pay for child care.

They will tell you to give up your dreams and go to work. They will say it's going to be too hard to care for a baby, go to school, and work at the same time. Why all the hate? Why all the negativity? It may be because of their own fears and insecurities about past failures they've experienced. Or it may be that they just don't believe you can be successful.

It will hurt to hear these words, especially from those you care about most. True, you may not have a high school diploma, but programs are available to help you earn a diploma or GED while going to college. True, you may not have money to go to school, but you can apply for financial aid, grants, and scholarships to help pay for college. True, you may not have child care, but certain organizations will help you find affordable child care. You'll find resources to help with these obstacles later in this book. You will read about specific programs to help you earn your high school diploma or GED, apply for financial aid, and choose and pay for quality child care. Also included in appendix A is a listing of colleges and universities that offer support services for student-parents such as on-campus housing, child care, and parenting groups.

Don't allow the haters to steal your joy. Remember to hold your head up high, stay positive, and focus on what you want. Even though the odds seem stacked against you, you can still go to college with a child. Tackle one challenge at a time until you remove each obstacle that seems to hold you back. Believe that all things are possible. Share your dreams with others. Not everyone is a hater. You will find a friend, a family member, or maybe a stranger who believes in you. You can do it. You can go to college. Give the haters a reason to become your biggest supporters. Prove them wrong and go to college.

Who has tried to discourage you, and how did that make you feel?

Keeping it REAL

_____

_____

_____

_____

_____

_____

_____

_____

_____

_____

_____

_____

_____

HATERS (continued)

Who are your supporters and how do they help?

_____

_____

_____

_____

_____

_____

_____

_____

_____

_____

_____

_____

_____

_____

_____

_____

_____

_____

_____

_____

_____

_____

Keeping it REAL

Professor, May I Bring My Baby to Class?

Are you ready to be inspired? Read these real-life stories of mothers who understand how important college was for themselves and their children. They faced many obstacles and haters who tried to stand in their way, but they didn't give up on their college goals.

Meet Talia

When people ask me how I manage to go to school as a single mother, I look at them with confusion. They must not understand how a woman feels when she looks at her children: How much guilt she has that, like her, they are growing up in a single-parent home. How she wants so much to give them the life they deserve. This devotion is an immeasurable push from within that could make her jump across a whole ocean if she had to.

Talia Barrows is a mother whose strength to continue her education is drawn from her children.

Women like us manage because we don't have a choice, like my daughter, who was unfairly born with cerebral palsy, has no choice. She fights every day to keep up with kids that can play more than she can, eat normally, or even go to the bathroom without help. She struggles with teachers who don't understand what she is going through and don't have time to help her. Or like my son, who wants to have his dad back. He doesn't have a choice but to live with a broken heart. He wants to play outside like some of his friends get to, but he can't because it is not safe. Watching his quiet disappointment or the way he takes care of his little sister like a parent himself keeps a fire burning inside me throughout the day and night.

Without them, I might not value my education like I do. And because of them I will never fail.

When I look at my kids, I know there is no choice for me. In my mind, my degree is already completed. They push me to match their bravery and accomplishments. We work together as we climb out of our struggles. Without them, I might not value my education like I do. And because of them I will never fail. They have already made me a success.

Talia Barrows graduated from Temple University in the spring of 2009 with a bachelor's degree in fine arts. She lives in Philadelphia, Pennsylvania, with her two children, Genero and Gesana. Talia believes that dance and other art forms should be utilized as tools for social change. She wants to create arts programming for school-age children to promote peace and political action in underprivileged communities. She plans to further her education by pursuing a master's degree in education.

Meet**Lautauscha**

At fifteen, a typical teenage girl should be worried about constructing a logical lie about why she couldn't get in by curfew on the night of the school dance or trying to convince her parents to give her a break from ballet since she's been going for over seven years. But at fifteen, I was worried about a lot more. I was worried if I'd qualify for the federal program WIC (Special Supplemental Nutrition Program for Women, Infants, and Children) to feed my child, if my son's father was messing around with other girls in the neighborhood, or if I could learn how to drive since getting on the bus with the stroller every day seemed impossible. Life was very different for me; I was not a typical teen in any respect.

Lautauscha Shell is a mother who saw the value of higher education in the jobs held by those who tried to hold her back.

Everywhere I looked people were giving me the "naughty little girl" looks because I was young, with a child. Old men were looking at me because they figured that I needed money to take care of my young child, and certainly I'd been having sex. Women looked at me like they just wanted to yell, "You don't know what you're in for." Then there were others who wouldn't look at me at all. My father glanced a few times, but seeing his baby girl with a baby boy was too much for him. My favorite aunt didn't look at me during visits to my grandmother's house because she didn't know what to say. My friends never looked at me the same way since I'd lost all of my credibility as their "Dr. Ruth." I felt like just another failed statistic—another girl who got pregnant, had a baby, and wouldn't amount to anything!

Professor, May I Bring My Baby to Class?

I still went on with my life; I couldn't just stop living. I couldn't change the fact that I was a teenage mom. I couldn't change the look on people's faces that spoke words of disappointment and disgrace, and I sure couldn't make my dad look at me like the baby girl I once was. But there was a look that brought peace into my life, a look that evoked motivation and courage: the look of my son's sweet face! I had given up the right to be shameful, depressed, lost, and confused. I had to make a plan. But what plan? What could I change about my life to stop the dirty looks? How could I show the world that I was not just another sad statistic? That I deserved another chance to be great?

As the story goes, I faced many woes. Going to school seemed more difficult for me as the days, weeks, and months passed. Juggling school, work, and a baby seemed doable for a short while, but eventually the juggling act began to collapse. The paychecks from McDonald's were just enough to cover the rent and phone bill, but only if I skipped school once a week to pick up extra hours at work. School was okay, but I couldn't

I knew that I wouldn't be a teenage mom forever, but I'd surely be poor forever if I didn't do something.

see the benefit of going every day. I didn't quite belong there anymore. So I made the choice to drop out of school and work full time. I had to support my kid, and school surely didn't provide diapers and milk.

Three years went by, and I worked and worked, sometimes earning enough to pay my rent, phone, and a little cable from time to time. I was taking care of my child, attending all of his doctor's appointments until one appointment when the receptionist informed me that my insurance had expired and that my child couldn't be seen by a doctor. What? Until this point, I had never realized how much control others had over my life. I always told my parents, my boyfriend, and even my boss at work that they couldn't control me. Now my baby's health and my sanity were in the hands of a welfare caseworker.

I knew that I wouldn't be a teenage mom forever, but I'd surely be poor forever if I didn't do something. But what? Every night I watched late-night shows about how to get rich. Other than the people on those shows, I didn't know anybody who was rich or even well-off. But what I did notice was that the majority of the professionals that I had come in contact with were college graduates. Mr. Novickus, my homeroom teacher who'd told me that he wasn't able to correspond with my other teachers to get my work when I'd missed classes while delivering my baby, had certainly gone to college. The caseworker, who told me that it was my responsibility to find a job that paid enough for me to take care of my child since I chose to have one, had to have gone to college. The director of the day care center that offered me a job paying a whopping fifty cents more than what I was earning at McDonald's had gone to college as well.

That was it! I was tired of feeling like a failure. Not only did I not earn enough money to take care of me and my child, I had yet another kid. That second trip to the birthing table is where I thought long and hard about the path I was taking, and that is when I decided to change my life. I decided to go to school since school was the only thing different about the lives of those that were able to take care of themselves.

As soon as my new baby turned three months old, I took the GED test and registered for college before I even had the results. I'd dropped out of school, but I was smart and I passed. When people ask how I did it, I say, "With a lot of paper and a pen." A monthly calendar with assignment dates, doctor's appointments, cleaning days, relaxing days, paydays, and what to pay on those days is how I managed being a student-parent for my undergraduate and graduate degrees.

This is a hard road to travel. It's not how hard the road is, but where it leads that is important. I now have a bachelor of science degree in elementary education, a master of social work degree, and am seriously considering a PhD program in the near future. Use the time and energy it takes to dwell on your teenage-parent status to figure out how to go to school, be a good mom, and you too will succeed. But, only with pen and paper will you be successful. If nothing else, write this down: "I will be successful, and I will break the cycle of poverty through education!"

Professor, May I Bring My Baby to Class?

Lautauscha Shell is a graduate of the University of Wisconsin–Milwaukee. She holds a master's degree in social work. She works as an after-school project director for the Kenosha Unified School District. She enjoys spending time with her family and often tells the students she works with that "limitations are self-imposed."

Meet Melissa

My name is Melissa. I am a thirty-two-year-old brown woman. I am a sister, a daughter, and most importantly a mother of four. I became a mother at the age of fifteen to my first son, who is now seventeen. By the age of sixteen I had my second child, a daughter. Their dad and I lasted about six years together before I had the courage to flee from him and his abuse.

Melissa Mendez-Arechiga is a mother who defied all odds to attend college.

When I heard about this opportunity to contribute to this book that might help or encourage someone else to pursue their education, regardless of what obstacles they face, I was extremely excited. I figured this would be easy, considering that I have been through so much. However, when I got down to writing my story, I realized it was not as easy as I thought. As I started to explore my past, a lot of feelings and emotions I never realized were there came to the surface. So it's been very difficult for me. This is the real deal—a glimpse into my life, my world, and my education.

I first introduced myself to you as a single mom with four children, but what I forgot to mention is that they are from three different baby's daddies. That's how we say it where I come from. Three different daddies who brought with them three different headaches. I didn't plan it that way, but that is just how it worked out. I never stopped to think about the hardship I had created for my children and myself. This would include emotional, financial, and educational hardship. Overall though, we are a pretty normal family—whatever that means.

But sometimes I wish someone would have cared enough to tell me to take school a little more seriously. Or that maybe a teacher would have seen my potential or noticed that I needed a little more support and given it to me. It could have made all the difference in my life.

Nevertheless, I am still standing strong and going forward with my education. I am currently a student at the University of California at Berkeley. Not bad for a kid who dropped out of school in junior high because I was too busy having babies instead of educating myself. The infamous saying comes to mind, "a baby having a baby." Yup. That was me all day long ghetto fabulous.

Being physically and mentally abused on a daily basis by the father of my oldest children eventually took its toll on me. What was more difficult for me to understand was that my family knew and did nothing to stop it. Upon social services stepping in to take away my children from me, it didn't matter that this man was four years older than me, making him an adult and me still a minor. Nor did the abuse my children and I suffered at his hands matter. Now it's my job to try to teach my children about not having babies at a young age. At the same time, I am still trying to move forward with my life and be an example to them and other young people who I cross paths with. Having kids young, being abused, dropping out of school, not knowing my father, and having a mother who was more concerned about partying than raising me were a few of the obstacles I faced in my preteen years. Despite the damage that all these experiences brought me, I learned to survive. To add to all these challenges, I made my life more difficult by becoming heavily involved with street gangs and, of course, drugs; the two go hand in hand. In no time I was on my way to prison because that also comes along with the lifestyle I chose. I had to face charges for carjacking, robbery, and kidnapping with a gun, which entitled me to a one-way trip upstate for twenty-five to life if I was convicted on all charges. Luckily, I walked away with only a three-year-and-eight-month sentence. So after twenty-five months I was released back into the world we call society. With nothing more than a GED that I got while in prison, my $200 gate money, and 500 duckets I had saved up from working PIA (Prison Industry Authority) after paying restitution to the courts, I left prison with my focus on getting my kids back. However, my bad attitude and prison rap sheet now pretty much guaranteed that no one would want to hire an ex-con much less an ex–gang member with tattoos on her face, neck, and—well—the whole body.

I had to face charges for carjacking, robbery, and kidnapping with a gun, which entitled me to a one-way trip upstate for twenty-five to life if I was convicted on all charges.

I quickly found my way back to the hood; I guess I never really left even though they locked me up. In no time I was back in the mix, hanging out and hooking up with one of the younger homies. It was a good match; we were like Bonnie and Clyde: we hung out together, we did dirt together, we got high together, but like all good things, it came to an end. We broke up, and I ended up driving myself to the hospital when I went into labor. He went on to get his bachelor's degree in engineering and went on living as if his child and I didn't exist.

A few years later I gave birth to my last and final child. I spent the next year or so as a homemaker. I depended on my husband to support me and the two little ones. (The two oldest were still with their father.) After a lot of disagreements, we also separated. I had no way to pay the rent and support my kids even with getting county benefits. We became homeless about a month later. My two little kids and I found refuge in a homeless shelter in San Pedro called Harbor Interfaith. In order for us to stay there, I needed to work or go to school and save 80 percent of my money so, when we left in three months, we would have enough money for an apartment. I agreed, and besides, the county expected the same effort from me as well. I figured I would be better off going to school than working—besides who would hire an ex-chola for any decent job with good pay? Honestly though, I really thought I was running game on the county.

When I started school at Los Angeles Harbor College in Wilmington, I was not sure what to expect. I really had just planned to cruise my way through until something else came along because I didn't believe in myself, and more importantly, I didn't understand that education is key to opening doors of opportunity. I lacked confidence in myself at first because of all that I had been through, plus I was going through a divorce, and my ex-husband was using my past against me because he wanted custody of my youngest child in order to avoid paying child support. The same old stuff: "She is an ex–gang member, she has had her eldest kids taken away, and she's been in prison." He tried everything and anything he could think of to make me look bad in the eyes of the court, and it worked. Even the judge told me with a sarcastic tone, "Mrs. Mendez, when you're actually doing something with your life, then you can worry about seeing your son on the weekends." Hence, my ex got custody of our son on the weekends despite threats against him by his girlfriend. It was an awful feeling to be treated as a joke in a courtroom. That

I decided to make things work for me. I became involved at school and found myself a job on campus.

feeling left me with a new perspective about my education and how the court system treats people like me. I remember telling that judge I would prove him wrong about me; he humiliated me in front of the whole courtroom and my ex-husband and his new girlfriend. I could not believe it; however, it seems as if things have worked against me my whole life. I decided to make things work for me. I became involved at school and found myself a job on campus. I started working in the counseling department. I loved learning all the ins and outs of how to make stuff happen for myself and others. Before long I established a good rapport with some faculty who gave me encouragement. After getting through my first semester, I realized that school wasn't that bad, and I could do it plus get paid. I was like, "This is dope, homie; I'm sold!"

As time progressed, I understood that I had the resources to try to obtain custody of my two eldest children. And I won. I got them back after ten years of not having them. Even though I had bounced back and forth between men, housing issues, and money issues, I succeeded in getting my kids back. Professors wrote letters to the judge explaining they were aware of my past history but that I was deserving to be a mother again to my two oldest. We won. I won. For once in my life, I got a taste of what victory felt like because of my education.

As I took each step, little did I know the possibilities that lay at my feet by simply going to school. All my life I figured that there had to be some other way—a special way to tap into what I thought was the American dream. How do I get my slice of apple pie? I've come to realize that, because I have figured out how to change my circumstances, I needed to share it with everyone. I also understand that some will listen while others may not, and some may try and knock me down because I am a new breed that society is not ready for. But I'm coming, whether they like it or not, to speak the truth about education to the future generations, because if I don't, who will?

Hopefully, this encourages you, no matter what your struggle is. You are not alone, and there are other women out there fighting the fight, breaking ground on your behalf. All you need to do is follow the trail we have left for you because the map is in your hands. Education is the only way! There are no short cuts to breaking free from the things you see in your own life that you hate.

> *Education is the only way! There are no short cuts to breaking free from the things you see in your own life that you hate.*

May you be encouraged, and if nothing else, I hope a seed of resolution has been planted within your heart forever.

Melissa Mendez-Arechiga is a student at the University of California, Berkeley. She was born and raised in Los Angeles, California, but currently resides in Albany with her four children: Ruben, Christina, Marissa, and Roman. Melissa is working hard to earn a dual degree in social welfare and American studies. She expects to graduate in May 2011. She loves listening to underground rap music. She aspires to continue her studies in law school on the East Coast. She dreams of working for peace in third-world countries.

Meet Deneisha

Me pregnant at sixteen just didn't make sense. I wasn't the type to have such a thing happen to me. I was shocked, and everyone in my family was too. When I started high school, I remember seeing girls pregnant at such a young age, and I vowed that that would never be me. I didn't want to be a statistic. So when I learned I was pregnant, I was devastated.

For as long as I could remember, I wanted to go to college. My friend and I decided early in high school that we were going to college in Virginia. Of course having my son, Jordan, at seventeen changed everything. My last year in high school was rough. I lost my mother in 2001 when Jordan was just five months old, and my relationship with Jordan's father was dwindling.

Even though my life was unstable, I enrolled in college in the spring of 2003 when Jordan was two years old. I worked while going to school to support myself and Jordan. Because I wasn't earning enough to take care of our needs, rent, and child care, three weeks before the semester ended, Jordan and I were homeless. I had to quit my job, and I couldn't finish the last three weeks of classes because I didn't have child care. Embarrassed, angry, hurt, and scared, Jordan and I went into the first of two shelters where we would live for the next six months. I applied for public assistance to support us.

While living in the first shelter, I met Polly, one of the workers. Polly was a huge inspiration to me and really supported me during my time in the shelters. The best advice she gave me was, "Prove them wrong." She was referring to the people around me that didn't believe I had what it took to succeed. This very simple advice has stuck with me throughout the years. Polly suggested the second shelter because it had a transitional housing program. If accepted into the program, we would have our own apartment for at least two years. Finally, Jordan and I would have a place of our own. We were accepted into

Deneisha Cauthen is a mother who is grateful for the woman she met at the homeless shelter.

Professor, May I Bring My Baby to Class?

the transitional housing program. Jordan was three by then and very happy to have his own room.

One night I remember praying to God for the chance to go to college full time and not have to worry about bills. Back in high school I had heard some girls talk about colleges that allowed you to live on campus with your children. After doing some research, I learned about Wilson College in Chambersburg, Pennsylvania. I applied, was accepted, and have been here for the past two years.

Going to school full time and being a full-time mother is challenging, but I've found techniques that work for us. I study when Jordan is sleeping at night. I still get stressed, but I press on, knowing the reward I am getting and giving to Jordan. I always knew I would go to college. After having Jordan, I knew it would just take me a little longer to get there. I am grateful to my sister, Deja, and cousin, Brenda, for their support during my journey.

I love the fact that Jordan is in a learning environment.

Living on campus with Jordan has been so rewarding. I love the fact that Jordan is in a learning environment. Most of all, I am pleased that I am being a positive influence in his life and showing him that education is rewarding. Knowing that I am teaching Jordan the value of education keeps me going. Now I know that it isn't just about proving others wrong, but more about proving myself right.

Deneisha Cauthen graduated from Wilson College in May 2009 with a bachelor's degree in psychology. While attending school, she and her son, Jordan, lived on campus in the residential housing for single mothers and their children. Deneisha enjoys photography and spending time with Jordan. She plans to attend graduate school and ultimately earn a doctorate in clinical psychology.

Meet**NaTasha**

Do you want to know how many people doubted that I would attend college? When I proved them wrong, their new argument was that I would not finish college. Do you know how many of my college peers, who had no responsibilities, said that I could not be a good student government vice president because I have a child? The answers to these questions are irrelevant. The people who doubt me do not matter. Everything that I have done since the time of conception has been for my son, Tashan.

NaTasha Goodman is a mother who is determined to prove her community wrong.

I attend Rosemont College, a small Catholic women's college in Pennsylvania. I have a three-year-old son. He is my motivation and my inspiration. His illuminating spirit is my conscience. His smile reminds me that I must complete my education. His laugh empowers me. I am forever in his debt, and because of that, I am going to be somebody. I am determined that my child will not grow up with lack of opportunity, as I did. I would like to dedicate my success to those who attempted to break my spirit. My eye is on the prize. I can assure everyone, positive and negative: I am not your average "college mom."

I will not sugarcoat anything. This journey has not been easy, and I don't plan for it to become easier anytime soon. Being a single parent is hard, but being a single poor parent, trying to better yourself is even harder. The welfare system is not college student friendly. It is designed for people who decide to attend trade schools. I have found it very difficult to obtain state assistance while in college. In order to be eligible for welfare assistance, it was mandatory for me to work at least twenty hours a week. They said that the welfare system only allowed a twelve-month school limit. The same issues arose with the child care department. My goal is not to collect welfare payments for the remainder of my life.

I do not want to live in dirty, drug-infested, crowded neighborhoods forever. I have moved every year while in college. I want to be able to provide stable housing for my son, and it hurts me that I struggle to do so. I understand that sacrifices must be made at times. As I said before, with every choice I make, my son's best interest is at heart. I refuse to keep jumping to the floor every New Year's Eve because people are celebrating the new year with gunshots. I am getting out of the ghetto. I have been here too long. I will not be brought down by it.

Being a mother is no easy task. Being a single mother and obtaining a college education requires a great deal of dedication. It is something your heart should be into! Nothing should stop you from reaching for the stars. A college mother's situation is not always understood, but I suggest that you still leave your signature while you are there. There will be professors or people who do not care about your personal life. Do not let that deter you from beginning or finishing.

There were days when I was forced to take my son to class with me. My professors did not like students to miss class. Some professors were actually happy that I decided to bring him. Others were appalled that I would even do such a thing. I did not care about what they thought. After

It is okay to cry; sometimes it is necessary to do so. We can thrive off of those who doubt us.

all, I was paying to be there. I wanted to show them that I had that drive that most people did not possess. I am sure to finish what I begin. I enjoy showing my competitive side. I have an alter ego. I am "tenacious Tasha." No one is going to dissuade me from engaging in my constitutional entitlement to the pursuit of happiness.

Keep this in mind. Stay focused on your parental development; this will be the foundation of your development. Do not ever let anyone tell you what you cannot or will not accomplish. No one decides your future but you. Smirk at the negativity thrown your way because it will continue to come as fast as the speed of light. Show everyone that mean words will not stop you. It is okay to cry; sometimes it is necessary to do so. We can thrive off of those who doubt us. It feeds our ego. Commend yourself often—you deserve it.

Appreciate those in your corner; a little support is better than none. You may be a statistic, but you're a role model to your child. You will finish school if you invest your time and talents wisely.

When graduation day comes May 16, 2009, my degree will be dedicated to those who caused me any sort of hardship as well as those who doubted me. I will be able to say, "Hi, I'm NaTasha Goodman. I possess a bachelor of arts degree, and I have phenomenal leadership abilities."

NaTasha Goodman and her active son, Tashan, live in Philadelphia, Pennsylvania. She is a proud graduate of Rosemont College, earning her bachelor's degree in May of 2009. NaTasha enjoys spending time with family and friends as well as mentoring young girls.

Meet La-Kee-a

My spirit was broken at a very early age. Trying to survive as a child growing up in the Fort Green housing projects in Brooklyn, New York, with drug-addicted parents was the reality of my life. Many children who share my story are thrust around from family members to strangers, forced to become adults before they're ready. Fortunately, my grandmother, like she had done so many times before with other relatives, took me in and raised me. It didn't matter that she could barely take care of herself, being paralyzed and stricken with polio. Her heart was full of love. She was my rock of inspiration.

By age thirteen, I was already working to help buy food and other necessities for our family. I never really got a chance to be a kid. Seeing my family struggle so much and trying to save us from the economic hardships of life was a burden no child should ever have to carry. Through all this, I managed to do well in high school and graduated at the top of my class. I always wanted to go to college. I knew it would save my life—take me out of poverty, out of the projects. I was going to be the first in my family to go to college.

La-Kee-a Lowry is a mother who learned to have hope by seeing through the eyes of her daughter.

I enrolled in Saint Michael's College in Colchester, Vermont, shortly after graduation. I quickly learned that I was not prepared for college or the culture. It was a different world for me. It was hard getting acclimated to my new surroundings. Trying to fit in at the majority-white school was even more traumatic. I experienced racism on many occasions. I could not keep up with the schoolwork, and I began to experience feelings of depression, inadequacy, and hopelessness. With no one to turn to for support, I soon dropped out.

After returning to New York for the summer, I learned my grandmother was now raising two other relatives, and the small two-bedroom apartment simply didn't have room for anyone else. I was homeless. While living in a convent on the Upper East Side, in Brooklyn, I was encouraged to go back to college. I attended Immaculata University in Pennsylvania, a small female college that changed my life and gave me hope. I had more support there; it felt like a home with family and security. Unfortunately, I became too comfortable with my new surroundings, going to parties off campus, meeting guys and hanging out with friends, not doing what I was supposed to do at school. I became pregnant that year, my grades suffered, and I again dropped out.

I made several attempts at suicide. But then the most beautiful thing happened. I had my daughter, Tatyana.

I moved in with my baby's father, who was abusive. The relationship didn't last long. The pain of bruised eyes and broken arms was more than I could bear. Although the injuries eventually healed, I would have permanent marks, and the emotional scars will be with me forever. Again, I was alone and miserable. Hopelessness settled in, and I fell into a deep depression and became isolated. I was convinced that God wanted me to be a failure. And I couldn't possibly take care of another human being. I could hardly take care of myself. I wasn't ready to become a mother. I made several attempts at suicide. But then the most beautiful thing happened. I had my daughter, Tatyana. Although she was diagnosed with epilepsy and would experience severe seizures, Tatyana saved my life. I love her more than anything in the world.

One day I met a stranger who invited me to her church. The church became my family. They helped me get into a transitional housing program. Soon, Tatyana and I would have our own home. With the support of my new church family and my faith in God, I began a beautiful journey of transformation. I had to confront my fears and pain of past hurts to begin the healing process of my broken spirit.

I gained the courage to once again enroll in college. This time, I attended Saint Joseph's University in Pennsylvania. I was older and wiser and became more focused on school and caring for Tatyana. My days and nights were consumed with visits to the hospital, school, and work. Many days I operated on three to four hours of sleep. On a number of occasions I had to take my daughter to class. Dr. Lavin, my journalism professor, insisted that I bring Tatyana to class. He did not want to see me fail or drop out of school again. Tatyana would sit quietly in the back of my class and color. I was grateful for his support. Later that semester, I was awarded a child care scholarship offered by Family Care Solutions, Inc. It was a blessing. I was able to enroll Tatyana in day care. I didn't have to worry about how I was going to pay for child care or who was going to watch her while I went to school. I could concentrate on finishing my degree. In 2004, I proudly earned my bachelor of arts degree in English and communications. I also graduated in life that year from the "university of fear," vowing never to turn back.

I want to give my daughter what I never had as a child—hope.

I want to give my daughter what I never had as a child—hope. I want her to dream and know that life is filled with possibilities and that she never has to limit herself by her circumstances. I realized that in order to provide a path for my daughter, I had to create a path for myself. I had the opportunity to visit Ghana and Egypt for a study tour while participating in a program at the African Genesis Institute. The experience changed my life forever. I decided to continue my education and enrolled in the international economic development master's program at Eastern University. I was persistent in identifying scholarships and grants to help me and Tatyana with our needs and was awarded a fellowship. I received financial aid to help with housing, transportation, and child care for my daughter. Looking back over my life, I never thought I'd be able to say that I have a master's degree. Tatyana and I graduated again in May 2008. She's been with me through it all, and she's been seizure free for the last five years. Today, we are on our way to Zambia, Africa. We're going to make a difference. I will be working in collaboration with local officials and radio stations to help educate and bring awareness to the people there about HIV and AIDS, the disease that plagues the country. We will also work to create economic and educational opportunities to local, marginalized citizens.

I want to encourage you not to give up, no matter what the circumstance. I learned how to persevere, and so can you.

La-Kee-a Lowry lives in Pennsylvania with her daughter, Tatyana. She graduated from Saint Joseph's University in 2004, earning a degree in communications and later from Eastern University in May 2008, earning a master's degree in economic development. La-Kee-a loves to read, travel, and help others. She aspires to reach for and achieve awesome heights, all through the glory of God.

CHAPTER 2

How Do I Prepare for College?

It's difficult going to school and caring for a baby, especially when you're a single parent. When your baby wakes up in the middle of the night, it's you who has to get up and console her. When you have no more diapers, it is likely you who will have to go out and get more. It's you who will drop him off at the child care center before going to school.

You seem to have no time to do fun activities anymore. You can't hang out with your friends like you used to. Having the responsibility of caring for another person is difficult. Sometimes you may feel happy and motivated; other times you may feel sad or angry. The only consistent feeling is exhaustion. It's okay to have all these emotions. Hang in there. Stay in school. Later in life, you will come to appreciate the hard times you spent getting through high school and college, especially when you purchase your first home or take a vacation in the Bahamas.

The biggest secret in life is that there is no big secret. Whatever your goal, you can get there if you're willing to work.

Oprah Winfrey

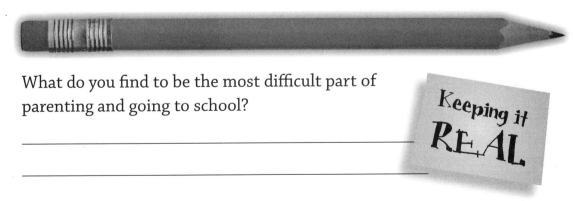

What do you find to be the most difficult part of parenting and going to school?

Keeping it REAL

_____

_____

_____

Keeping it
REAL

_____
_____
_____
_____
_____
_____
_____
_____
_____

WHAT TYPE OF COLLEGE IS RIGHT FOR ME?

What you want to become will determine what type of degree, professional certificate, or license you will need. The country has over 9,000 colleges, universities, and career schools to help you prepare for your future.[1]

WHAT'S THE DIFFERENCE?

A *college* is a four-year institution awarding a bachelor's degree. Students may choose colleges that serve a specific population, for example, women's and men's colleges, historically black colleges and universities, Hispanic colleges, and religious colleges.[2]

A *university* includes a college as well as a graduate school and one or more professional schools, such as a medical school or law school. Students attending a university may pursue a bachelor's degree (four years of schooling), a master's degree (two years beyond the bachelor's degree), a doctorate (PhD) or professional degrees.[3]

Attending a college or university opens the door to endless possibilities in areas of study. Some careers available to those with a college or university degree include but are not limited to these:

- Civil attorney
- Registered nurse
- Chemical engineer
- Educator
- Advertising executive
- Psychologist
- Economist

- News anchor
- Physical therapist
- Teacher
- Accountant
- Dentist
- Forensic scientist
- Pharmacist
- Veterinarian

> **DID YOU KNOW?**
>
> A college graduate will earn nearly $1 million more over a lifetime than a high school graduate.[4]

A *community* or *junior college* offers educational and training programs leading to an associate degree in two years or a license or certificate in less than two years. Many people start their education at a two-year college and then transfer to a four-year college or university and apply their credits toward earning a bachelor's degree. Many career choices are available at two-year schools to prepare you for the workplace.[5] Here are just a few:

- Professional dancer
- Law enforcement officer
- Early childhood education

- Clinical lab technician
- Graphic designer
- Dental hygienist[6]

A *career school* offers job-specific training that provides real work experience. You can earn a degree or certificate at a career school. When you graduate from a career school, you will already know what to do on your new job.[7] You may attend a career school to become qualified to work in one of these jobs:

- Medical assistant
- Court reporter
- Animation art designer

- Chef
- Physical therapist aid
- Fashion designer[8]

Some of these career choices may also be found at a community or junior college.

Most colleges and universities offer distance education or on-line learning to meet the demands of busy people.[9] These educational options are becoming more and more popular among people who don't want to give up a job and salary while they are in school, live far from the college, or have young children. Students learn their subject matter using primarily the Internet. On-line learning allows you to access your classes and lessons twenty-four hours a day, seven days a week from any computer with Internet access.

CHOOSING YOUR MAJOR

Once you have narrowed down the type of college, university, or career school you want to attend, make a list of the specific programs that interest you. Look at what courses you will be expected to take if you choose that program. For example, a person interested in becoming a pharmacist should like chemistry. She will have to take a lot of chemistry classes. A person interested in becoming an accountant should like math. She'll be working with numbers constantly in her career.

You can choose from hundreds of courses and career choices. Whatever you decide to study at college will become your major. If you are interested in two careers, you may have a minor as well. For example, if marketing is your first career choice and music your second, marketing will become your major and music your minor.

Thousands of Web sites provide information about career choices at colleges and universities and career schools. Visit the Web sites of the schools you are interested in attending to learn about their academic programs, the majors they offer, their admissions processes, campus life, student population, and more. See appendix A for a few Web sites that provide information about career choices.

I am interested in attending a (choose from the types of colleges listed on pages 32 and 33)

Keeping it _REAL_

_____

because . . .

_____

_____

_____

_____

_____

_____

_____

_____

I plan to major in _____

to become a _____ .

I chose this career because

_____

_____

_____

_____

_____

CHOOSING A REPUTABLE SCHOOL

When considering a school, always make sure the institution or program is accredited by a respected and recognized organization. Accreditation means that the school has met standards of quality to ensure your degree has value. This is particularly important when you graduate and begin looking for a job. Your potential employer will want to know if your degree is valid. Also, a school that is accredited is eligible to participate in the federal student aid program, which means that you can apply for financial aid to attend that school. Some programs that do not award degrees may also be accredited by a respected agency.[10]

Be careful of fake degrees—"degree mills" or "accreditation mills."[11] Before you call that number that's flashing across the television screen or that appears in your e-mail, learn more about what to look for when considering a program. Unfortunately, some people will trick you out of thousands of dollars and give you a degree that's not real. Know how much the entire program will cost before you start. If you're not careful, you could use up all your federal aid before the program is over, leaving you thousands of dollars in debt. This is particularly damaging if you want to transfer to another school. You won't be able to apply for federal aid because you've used it all up. You may also learn that your credits are not transferable, meaning other schools won't accept them. Spending some time now learning about a school or program might save you thousands of dollars later.[12]

When choosing a respected college or university make sure that it meets these criteria:

▶ The postsecondary institution you are interested in attending is accredited by a recognized accrediting agency or your state's Department of Education. (See appendix A for a list of Web sites of accrediting agencies and accredited institutions.)

▶ The school you are transferring to accepts the credits of the school you are transferring from.

▶ Your potential employer recognizes your degree as a valid credential.[13]

CHOOSING A COLLEGE WITH CHILD CARE SERVICES

Many colleges and universities offer great programs to help you become a successful student-parent. Over seventeen hundred child care centers are located on college campuses across the country.[14] In addition to child care, some offer on-campus housing for single parents and their children and financial assistance to help you pay for child care. Some schools have student-parent support groups that help promote activities and advocate for new services on campus for student-parents. The National Center for Education Statistics (NCES) and the National Coalition for Campus Children's Centers (NCCCC) are great resources to help you identify schools with on-campus child care centers. NCES has a more comprehensive list, whereas NCCCC lists only its member child care providers. You may request a list of these schools from both organizations. See appendix A for their Web sites.

DID YOU KNOW?

The Federal Trade Commission warns students to be cautious of information that includes statements like the following because they are likely to come from scammers:

- "The scholarship is guaranteed or your money back."
- "You can't get this information anywhere else."
- "I just need your credit card or bank account number to hold this scholarship."
- "We'll do all the work."
- "The scholarship will cost some money."
- "You've been selected by a 'national foundation' to receive a scholarship."
- "You're a finalist" in a contest you never entered."[15]

Avoid scholarship scams.

We've identified forty colleges and universities to help you get started on your search for on-campus student-parent support services. You will find them listed in a table in appendix A. Remember there are hundreds more. Using the list you requested from NCES or NCCCC, contact child care centers at colleges and universities in your area and create a similar chart. Start by asking these questions to learn more about other on-campus programs for student-parents:

▶ Does the school have an on-site child care center?

- Does the school offer services to help students find off-site child care?

- Does the school offer scholarships or grants to help pay for child care?

- Does the school have a student-parent support program or on-campus parenting group?

- Does the school have a campus office that specifically addresses student-parent and child care issues (for example, a women's center, student affairs office, or financial aid office)?

- Does the school offer housing for single parents and their children?

- Can children be transported using the school's shuttle bus service?

- Can a child accompany parents to the student dining hall?

APPLYING TO COLLEGE

In order to attend a college, you first must apply to the school by completing its admissions application. The admissions application provides information about you and the desired program of study you plan to pursue. Along with your admissions application you will have to submit your high school transcript or GED scores and test scores from one of the national standardized tests, the SAT or the ACT. The scores from these tests help determine if you are prepared for college. If your test scores show that you are not quite ready, the admissions counselor may suggest you take refresher courses before taking college classes. SATs and ACTs are offered several times a year. Courses and books are also available to help you prepare for these tests. See appendix A to learn where you can find more information about the SAT and ACT, such as help preparing for these tests, the costs, how to register to take the tests, and where to go to take them.

Some colleges can be very competitive. That means that so many qualified students apply each year that the schools have to choose which students they will accept. In this case, the admissions staff may look at more than just your application, grades, and entrance exam scores. They will also look at recommendations from your teachers and your extracurricular activities. As part of the process you could also be asked to write an essay and participate in an interview. An essay and interview will allow you to share personal information about yourself, your family, and why attending college is important to you. Each school's requirements are different. Go to the school's Web site for information about the application process.

RETURNING TO SCHOOL AFTER AN ABSENCE

Not sure if you are ready to jump right into the college scene? Community colleges are a great place to start your education if you dropped out of high school or are looking to return to school after a long absence. Many offer courses to help you sharpen your English, math, and reading skills before taking college courses. Programs are designed to fit your needs and your schedule. Anyone can go to a community college, regardless of previous academic experience. You can earn your high school diploma while earning college credits toward an associate degree or certificate.[17] It can be done, but you need to take the first step. Call the admissions office at your local community college and ask about programs to help you reenter school.

> **DID YOU KNOW?**
>
> Here are some facts about the student population at community colleges:
>
> - 60 percent are women
> - 39 percent are first-generation students (students who are the first in their immediate family to go to college)
> - 17 percent are single parents
> - 35 percent are minorities[16]

Two programs that can help you succeed in school are Gateway to College and Achieving the Dream. Gateway to College helps youth between the ages of sixteen to twenty who dropped out of high school earn their diploma and go to a community college.[18] Achieving the Dream is an initiative that holds community colleges accountable for a student's success. That means these colleges have accepted the challenge to do what is necessary to help you successfully graduate. They are particularly concerned about nontraditional students who face significant barriers to success.[19] (Hello, that's you—a single mom with little money!) Identify community colleges that offer these programs in your neighborhood. They are working hard to help you succeed. (See appendix A for their Web sites.)

Other programs may be available in your community to help you reengage in school, whether you are a few credits away from earning your diploma, GED, or college degree or looking to enroll in college for the first time. Search Google or your city's or state's Department of Education Web site to find programs in your area.

I plan to contact the following programs in my community to help me reenroll in school:

Keeping it REAL

_____

_____

_____

_____

_____

_____

_____

_____

I PLAN TO APPLY TO THE FOLLOWING COLLEGES:

Name of college/ university/career school	Application deadline	Transcript required? (yes/no)	Recom- mendations required? (yes/no)	Essay required? (yes/no)	Interview required? (yes/no)	SAT/ACT required? (yes/no)	Accepted? (yes/no)

PAYING FOR COLLEGE

Will higher education ever be free for all who want to go? If you live in Kalamazoo, Michigan, it already is. Philanthropists (generous rich people who donate money to worthy causes) who understand the importance of higher education and its impact on our economy, communities, and future have established a tuition-free program, the Kalamazoo Promise. The program pays up to 100 percent of college tuition for students who live in Kalamazoo and who have been enrolled in the public school system for at least four years. Unlike other tuition-free programs, which are based on grades and need and offered only to a certain group of students, the Kalamazoo Promise is available to any high school graduate wanting to go to college, regardless of her grades or financial status. Students can choose among forty-four public state universities or community colleges to attend in the state of Michigan.[20] Wouldn't it be wonderful to have this opportunity anywhere in America?

If you don't live in Kalamazoo, your first thoughts about college are probably, How much does it cost, and can I afford it? Whether people are rich, poor, purple, or green, college should be accessible and affordable to all who desire to go. However, your family's income and your ability to get additional aid may determine where you can go to college.

ACCESSING FINANCIAL AID

To get financial aid, you should start by completing the Free Application for Federal Student Aid (FAFSA) form on-line.[21] This application will determine how much financial aid you are eligible for and what types of aid will be awarded. You can receive three types of financial aid—grants, loans, and work study (students earn money through part-time employment to help them pay for their education). Your financial status and possibly also your parent's financial status will determine your need for financial assistance. Once you complete the FAFSA form, and it has been processed, written comments on your Student Aid Report (SAR) will inform you if you have to provide proof of income (taxable or nontaxable income).[22] Schools use the information from your FAFSA application to determine how much additional aid you will need to cover the full cost of attending their schools. Each school you are accepted to will prepare a financial aid package to show you how much money you will receive from them. The package includes a financial aid award letter detailing the amount of money you will receive in the form of federal, state, and school aid. Unlike a loan that you have to pay back, grants and scholarships are gifts—you don't have to repay them.[23]

You may find that when you get your package you will still need more money to cover tuition and fees.[24] If your parents can't afford to pay the remaining balance, and you attend a school that does not offer need-based grants, you may need to take out a student loan. The word "loan" is a turnoff to many people. But there is absolutely nothing wrong with taking out a loan to help pay for college.

When I was discussing paying for college with a group of teens, one young mother said she didn't want to take out a loan for school because she planned to get a car.

"Let's think about this for a minute," I said. "A loan for a new car or an education? How are you going to pay for that car loan?"

How can you compare the value of a new car that depreciates the day you drive it off the lot to the long-term value of an education? The value of a college degree is a much greater investment than a car. Look for low-interest loans that you don't have to begin to pay back until after graduation. Talk to the college financial aid counselor for more information about student loans. See appendix A for Web sites that discuss types of loans.

FAFSA forms are available each January first for the upcoming academic year. To take advantage of college scholarships and state grants, complete and submit the FAFSA form on-line early in the year. Since schools and states have different deadlines, it's important to know the deadlines so you don't miss out on available money.[25] Funds are usually awarded on a first-come, first-served basis. So when the money is gone, it's gone. Ask the college financial aid officer about school deadlines for grants and scholarships. See appendix A for Web sites to access and apply for federal aid and to learn more about your SAR and state deadlines.

NEED-BASED GRANTS

Many colleges and universities have established need-based grants to help low-income students pay for their educations. Need-based grants may replace your parents' contributions and student loans, making it free money you don't have to pay back.[26] Guess what? You can even apply for a need-based grant at high-priced schools like Harvard, Yale, and Princeton.[27] You can go to these schools and others like them for free or next to nothing, depending on your family's income. How wonderful not to have any school loans after graduation.

It took me twelve years to repay my school loan. For others it can take twice as long and longer.

The requirement for these grants differs from school to school. Start by asking the financial aid counselor the questions listed below. Asking these questions will help you determine (1) if you are eligible for a need-based grant, (2) the amount of money you are eligible to receive, and (3) if the amount you are eligible for doesn't cover the full cost, the amount of other contributions you will have to make.

- How much are tuition and fees?
- Does the school offer need-based grants?
- What are the school's requirements to apply for a need-based grant?
- Based on your income, will your tuition and fees be 100 percent covered?
- If not, how much will your need-based grant cover?
- Will you be required to take out student loans to support your need-based grant?
- Will you be required to work to support your need-based grant?
- Are your parents expected to make a contribution?
- As a student-parent, can you apply independently of your parents?
- If yes, how do you do that?
- What other scholarships or grants can you apply for?
- When is the deadline for applying for other financial aid?

Not interested in going to a four-year school? Community colleges are generally the least expensive of all colleges and universities, making them a bargain.[28] To save money, many people start at a local community college, earn an associate degree, and then transfer their credits to a four-year college or university to earn a bachelor's degree. Ask your school about a dual admissions program. This program is an agreement between the community college and a four-year college or university that allows you to transfer without going through the normal process of transferring. That means you will be able to avoid application and transcript fees and become eligible for scholarships. If you maintain a certain GPA (grade point average), all your credits are likely to transfer, giving you junior status at your new school.[29]

Public schools cost less than private colleges and universities. They get most of their money from federal and state governments. Public schools generally have a larger student population. Private schools rely heavily on research funding, alumni support, and student tuition to fund their schools. They tend to be smaller than public schools.[30]

It really doesn't matter where you decide to go to school. Higher learning is rewarding at any of America's colleges and universities. What matters most is that you get a great education that will lead to a fulfilling career. Whether it's at a community college or at a public or private college or university, higher education will change your life and your child's life.

PRIVATE SCHOLARSHIPS AND GRANTS

A great place to start looking for money for college is right in your own backyard. No, a hidden treasure is probably not buried there, so don't start digging. Your school counselor, family, friends, and community organizations can be great resources for helping you identify money for college.

Ask your parents to check with their employers to see if they offer scholarships and grants to children of employees. Ask friends if they could identify other friends who are in college and willing to share the resources they used to access scholarships and grants. Your neighborhood churches, synagogues, and other places of worship may have scholarships for their members and their members' families. Contact your state senator's or state representative's offices to inquire about scholarships and grants as well. Go to your state's department of higher education Web site for a listing of state-funded scholarships and grants.

You should also contact the financial aid office at the college or university you are interested in attending and ask about alumni-established scholarships you may qualify for. Many alumni give back to their alma maters (the school they graduated from) by establishing scholarships to help others. These scholarships can be awarded to students based on financial need, college major, race, athletic ability, religious affiliation, extracurricular activities, or academics, depending on the scholarship.[31] Academic scholarships are also known as merit-based aid. Search Google for scholarships and grants that match your interests. For example you can Google "scholarships for women in nursing," "scholarships for women in sports," or "scholarships for women with children." You get the idea. Sororities are also great resources for scholarship opportunities.

Warning! You should never have to pay anyone to help you find money for college.[32] Many nonprofit organizations offer free advice and services to help you search for money for college. The Internet is a wonderful tool to help you find these organizations. Search Google for college access programs that are in your area and that can give you assistance and referrals.

It's hard for people to believe my story when I share how I got money to finish my last year of college through a car dealership. As I always say, nothing is impossible.

When I was in my last year of college at the University of Maryland, I was told I had exceeded my limits for financial aid and I couldn't apply for any more Pell Grants or loans at the school. If I couldn't come up with the tuition for my last semester, I couldn't finish school. I was devastated. I had come too far to stop at that point.

I couldn't just drop out of school. No one else in my family had graduated from college. I had to be the first—to set an example for my younger siblings and to make something of myself.

Driving home one evening, I began to think about all that I'd gone through to get where I was and how I had already struggled for over five years in college. What was I going to do? Where was I going to get the money to finish college? As I cried and prayed, something inside me said, "Turn here, turn here." I did, and it was a car dealership. Just as I pulled closer to the dealership's door, an idea came to me—go inside and ask for a scholarship. How crazy was that thought?

I did. I asked the man sitting behind the desk if they gave out scholarships. He looked at me as if I was a little "off" and simply said, "No, we don't give out scholarships here. This is a car dealership. See, look around." I stared at him for a few seconds with tears streaming down my face. I could only imagine what he was thinking as I sat there, embarrassed and afraid to move.

He gave in and asked, "What's wrong?"

I told him the story.

He said again, "We don't give out scholarships young lady, but I happen to know someone who works in the financial aid office at the University of Maryland." He made a phone call while I was there.

I got the money I needed to finish college and graduated in May 1986 with a bachelor of science degree in electrical engineering. Okay, you can say it. Did that really happen? Yes, it did, and I have pictures and a roommate to prove it!

If you're not as bold as I am, or you don't care to try my crazy idea, see appendix A for a list of Web sites of organizations and businesses that offer scholarships and grants to women, students, single mothers, and student-parents. Remember, hundreds of additional opportunities are available in addition to these.

What challenges are you currently faced with that seem impossible to conquer?

_____

_____

_____

_____

_____

_____

_____

_____

_____

_____

What actions are you taking to help overcome these challenges?

_____

_____

_____

_____

_____

_____

_____

Professor, May I Bring My Baby to Class?

ACTIONS (continued)

_____

_____

_____

_____

_____

_____

Keeping it REAL

How are these actions working out for you?

_____

_____

_____

_____

_____

_____

_____

_____

_____

_____

_____

_____

_____

Are you ready to be motivated? Read these real-life stories of mothers who kept it real. They thought about dropping out of school, and a few did, only to return years later. Others decided to go back to school after concluding that they and their children deserved more in life.

Meet**Anna**

I was dirty and wild and sometimes, perhaps most of the time, uncontrollable. But I had a drive and ambition that told my parents I wouldn't stop until I had succeeded at whatever endeavor I attempted.

Anna Connors is a mother who had too much potential to consider dropping out of school.

I was a good student, getting mostly As throughout school, and crying when I got below a B, which wasn't often. It was always important to me, my education. I knew that I needed to make the most of it if I wanted to amount to anything in life, at least anything I deemed worth amounting to.

At the age of fifteen, I thought I'd found Mr. Right, and shortly after my sixteenth birthday I found out I was pregnant. I had gone to the clinic for a booster of the birth-control shot, and my mother, who knew about my sexual relations, thought it would be a good idea to get all the other female tests out of the way—smears and pokings and whatnot.

I was sitting in my exam room in the clinic afterwards, and nibbling on the end of my pen waiting for the nurse with the needle to come in. The nurse came in with a folder and a solemn, sympathetic look on her face. She sat down across from me, and I could tell that something was wrong. Then she told me I was pregnant.

There was a clatter as my pen dropped to the table, and for a moment I was speechless. Were they sure? Well, yes, they'd run the test when they felt a suspicious lump in my belly.

I sat stunned, and finally, cowardly asked the nurse if she could tell my mother, who was in the waiting room. I described her to the nurse, and she left the room. Shortly, I could hear my mother's abrasive voice in the next room, reaming the nurse out, as if the nurse was the one who'd impregnated me. I felt horrible for shirking the responsibility and putting it on her, but in that moment I felt so weak and so young.

What ensued was a battle of authority between my mother and me. I was an adult—I felt so, but she wouldn't listen to me. On my own, I struggled to find the answers to the situation. It was only a puzzle, and I had only to find the right pieces, and the picture would become clear. I'd always been good at that. But this particular battle was not just about me anymore, and that was what I found the most difficult.

I started my junior year of high school, harboring the bitter secret. Over time, as my belly began to grow large, and my joints began to ache from the pressure, I took to wearing looser clothing and sweaters. I didn't want anyone to know that I had made a mistake.

After school I would come home and lie down on my bed, turn toward the wall, and I would cry and sleep and wake up to cry some more. If my mother came into my room, I would ignore her or yell at her to leave me alone. I ceased to care about school or my health or the future and lived only with the quiet dread that filled me as the baby grew within me.

My dad and stepmother thought it best if I moved in with them. My mother didn't fight me when I started packing to move.

Somehow, despite all the emotional turmoil and family struggles, things weren't really that bad. I wasn't ready to have a child, I knew that, but what frightened me the most was that I would have to drop out or go to school an extra year. One day, I sat down with my student advisor and explained my situation to her. Together, we looked over my records and talked about my options. Because I was such a hard-working student, I had extra credits built up. These extra credits enabled me to fulfill several requirements, and I basically skipped a grade. (Although the school refused to acknowledge me as a senior, I was a junior taking senior-level courses.)

One teacher in particular, my U.S. history teacher, was really helpful. He saw my potential, and when I told him why I couldn't go on that year's history trip to Alabama, his face fell. But he was determined to help me succeed. A group of friends and I started eating lunch in his classroom, where we would talk about all sorts of things, from history to politics, to music and movies. It was always a laugh, but it was his network of support that I needed.

My parents would have allowed me to stop going to school at any point I felt it was too much to handle, but up until three days before the baby was born, I waddled through the hallways. I knew I'd be gone for a while, and I didn't want to risk falling behind. I met with all my teachers privately and gathered all the work I would need for the following month. I left my e-mail address with them and told them who my student contact would be so she could bring me anything I needed.

When my baby was born, I was filled with an overwhelming sense of relief and love. I had gone through so much, and now she was in the world with me, and I loved her incredibly. It all seemed worth it.

I bounced back pretty well. I was tired, but it didn't have an effect on my daily routine. Being so young, I was used to staying up eighteen hours a day and rushing from one thing to another. But my daughter was so quiet and happy that I didn't get stressed out very much. At times, I would bring out my textbooks, lay her down next to me, and begin to read aloud to her. She would listen intently until she fell asleep. Using that as my method for studying, I didn't fall behind in school.

I returned to school when she was six weeks old. Thanks to my parents' support, I was able to get her into a good child care center. My teachers and friends worked with me until I caught up. I think they were so willing and eager to help me succeed because I was so eager to do it. Other teen parents in my school either didn't return to school or returned but didn't have enough hope in the future to keep trying. But my teachers saw in me the drive to keep going.

So at the end of my junior year, I walked across the stage with the seniors, received my diploma, and that summer I was accepted into a nearby college as an anthropology student. My struggles didn't go unnoticed, and I was chosen to receive a scholarship that would cover my tuition expenses for my first year and, depending on financial need, the rest of my years in school.

It was hard, and it felt like a completely uphill battle, but I couldn't stop fighting. I wanted to go to school more than anything, and I wasn't going to let anything else get in my way. Looking back now, two years later, I wouldn't change a thing. It was a needed experience. I've grown so much since then, and I've learned how to handle rough, seemingly hopeless situations. I've built a web of support; it includes my parents, friends, advisors, and old and current professors. The latter are probably the most helpful, because establishing a sort of friendship with them has helped them understand my situation so that if I need to skip class because my daughter is sick, they don't think I'm being disrespectful. They are also more willing to help me out if I begin to fall behind.

> *It was hard, and it felt like a completely uphill battle, but I couldn't stop fighting. I wanted to go to school more than anything, and I wasn't going to let anything else get in my way.*

I adore my daughter, and I'm thankful for her because if it hadn't been for her, I probably wouldn't have achieved so much. She closed the door to my carefree childhood, but it seems like she's opened a million more windows that point to so many great opportunities I wouldn't have had otherwise.

Anna Connors graduated from the University of Wisconsin–Milwaukee in December 2008 with a degree in anthropology. She is currently traveling the country working as a storyteller. Anna plans to enroll in graduate school in September 2010. She wants to create archaeology and anthropology programs for children using interactive methods such as theatre and mini-archaeological digs. Anna credits her success to her daughter. They enjoy spending time playing, going places, and just being together.

Meet Jessica

Being a twenty-one-year-old brings about its own set of problems. But being twenty-one with a four-year-old to care for creates a whole new genre of problems. I was a sixteen-year-old in high school and still angry at my parents for moving us from my childhood town in San Diego to the San Francisco Bay Area. I had put a great deal of effort into my relationship with my first boyfriend. He seemed like the perfect guy, and I thought I was in love, until the day I began to hear rumors about him messing around with other girls. Being naive, I chose not to listen to my friends, but in the back of my mind I had that feeling of insecurity. I became pregnant later that year with his child. He decided that he did not want to be involved in my child's life, and I felt like I was all alone.

Jessica Jamora is a mother who stayed in school to make her son proud.

The timing couldn't have been worse. My only brother had passed away just a few months earlier. I was very worried about what my father's reaction would be when he found out I was pregnant. His baby girl was having his first grandchild. I knew he would be disappointed and heartbroken.

Feeling forced to have an abortion by my boyfriend, I called Planned Parenthood. For some strange reason they would not pick up the phone. I tried calling and calling but never received an answer. I finally gave up and decided to call the next day. That night I had a dream that changed my life. In my dream, my brother spoke to me and encouraged me not to have an abortion. I didn't. Eight months into my pregnancy not a single person had figured out what was going on except for my older sisters. Jadyn was born August 26, 2003. He was a blessing and brought my family closer together.

Going back to school for my senior year after giving birth was not a fun thing to look forward to. I got a great deal of stares, and people did not treat me the same as before. My friends were not the same, and I felt like an outsider. I decided that school was not the route for me. I cut classes all the time, threatening my chance to graduate high school on time. Realizing my son needed me to be successful, I changed my behavior and decided I had to finish high school. I had to become something better for Jadyn. I wanted him to be proud of the woman his mother would eventually become. It was definitely a challenge. My parents didn't make a lot of money and could barely support our family. So supporting myself and Jadyn was tough. I did not want us to live in poverty our entire lives.

After graduating high school, I attended junior college for two-and-a-half years and then transferred to San Francisco State University. Through perseverance and love from my family, I see that nothing is impossible if you truly fall in love with it.

Jessica Jamora graduated from San Francisco State University in May of 2009 with a bachelor's degree in psychology. She cherishes her memories of going to school with Jadyn. She plans to continue her education. Jessica enjoys spending time with her family and her son, Jadyn.

Meet**Sandra**

So if I make macaroni and cheese for dinner with apples on the side, he will at least get some fruit today, and it would only take me fifteen minutes to prepare. But in order for him to go to bed at 7:30 p.m., he has to finish dinner at 6:00 p.m. so that I can then give him a bath and play with him. I have to be at home by at least 5:00 p.m. Focus Sandra, focus. The bottom squared, then the bottom times the derivative of the first minus—and don't forget the parenthesis—first times the derivative of the bottom . . . quotient rule . . . Okay, I think I got it.

Sandra Simon is a mother whose son inspired her to go to college years later.

$$\frac{d}{dx}\left[\frac{f(x)}{g(x)}\right] = \frac{g(x)\dfrac{d}{dx}[f(x)] - \left(f(x)\dfrac{d}{dx}[g(x)]\right)}{[g(x)]^2}$$

These are the thoughts that run through my head most days. A jumble of family life, mundane responsibilities, schedules, schoolwork, backup schedules, more schoolwork, emergency schedules, homework, potty training, money, lack of money, which supermarket has the specials on my son's favorite fruit this month, and how to accomplish all this in only a twenty-four hour period. I am a full-time student and a full-time parent. I look at my life, and I see a chaotic mess that would drive the messiest person to the brink of insanity, and yet I would not have it any other way.

It all started one day when I saw myself reflected in the eyes of my innocent one-year-old. There I sat—single, broke, and with a small child staring at me with all the trust in the world. As I saw myself in his eyes, I took a good look at my life and realized that I was going nowhere.

I had never felt so grateful for the innocence, faith, and trust in my son's eyes.

What life could I offer him? When had I stopped believing in my dreams? What had happened to the spunky little ten-year-old girl who told her father that one day she would help save the world? It was then that I realized that I had to change if I wanted to be that girl again.

I was terrified. I didn't know what to do. I thought that there was no way that I could go to college after all these years and fulfill a dream I could barely remember. So I did the only thing I could do: I started at the beginning. Looking back, I realize that no matter how hard I think life is right now, nothing was harder than taking the first steps in the process. I actually had to fill out three applications because I was so nervous I completely ruined the first two. Yet, I wasn't finished; I still had to finish the next step. I had to enroll and attend class. Every day, before classes started, became a challenge. I continuously debated whether I really needed to go. I knew in my mind that it was the logical thing to do, but terror gripped my heart. I felt like it was a gamble, a risk almost too great to take.

I always look at that point in my life and smile. I smile because, even though it was the hardest decision I ever made, I had never felt

Professor, May I Bring My Baby to Class?

so grateful for the innocence, faith, and trust in my son's eyes. It was his utter belief in my being able to provide for him that made me ignore my doubts and insecurities while forging ahead. The first day of class was indeed scary. I felt like I was five years old all over again, screaming that I didn't want to go to kindergarten and that I wanted to go home. I felt so out of place. It wasn't that I was much older than some of the people there, but in my mind I felt I was light years away. I had a child and with that came the worries and responsibilities of being a parent.

It has now been over a year and a half that I have been back in school, and I still feel awkward in school and like I have very little in common with most students. But I have found that it isn't as bad as I had thought it was going to be. My single most constant motivating factor in my life is the trust my son has in me. It is this feeling that lets me stay up that extra hour to study when I am exhausted. I can't say it is easy, but I can say that it is easier than those first steps. As for fitting in, I won't be winning any popularity contests, but I have found that the situation isn't as dark as it seemed to be. The classes are filled with friendly people from all walks of life who have just as many worries as me, only of a different kind.

Now it just seems routine, going to school. I wake up, and I can't imagine what made me have those feelings of fear, but I am glad I ignored them and kept moving forward. I see a future that I look forward to reaching, filled with possibilities and the remnants of that ten-year-old girl, and I have never been happier.

Sandra Simon and her son live in Milwaukee, Wisconsin. She attends the University of Wisconsin–Milwaukee and expects to graduate in the spring of 2010 with a bachelor's degree in chemistry and a minor in mathematics. Sandra enjoys reading, dancing, and cooking.

Meet**Jessica**

My son was born when I was fifteen years old, a sophomore in high school. I stayed in school and graduated in 2004. I knew it would be difficult to go away to college. So I applied to and was accepted at a two-year college closer to home. I studied to become an x-ray technologist. My years in school were the most strenuous years of my life. It was extremely difficult to juggle my time between school, family, work, and friends.

A normal day for me would start around 6:00 a.m., getting myself and James ready in the morning, eating breakfast, dropping him off at day care, and finally going to clinical and classes for the day. After classes I would go to work for a few hours and then pick James up from day care right before it closed at 6:00 p.m. Dinnertime was quality time for James and me even if he was throwing the food instead of eating it. When I tried to do homework or just sit and study, he would climb all over my lap trying to rip my papers. He needed his mom's attention even if he got it for being in trouble.

Some days it was almost impossible to go to school, work, and be a mom all in one day. It was hardest to leave James on the days he got sick. One morning he vomited cereal and apple juice all over my homework right before I had to leave for school. When I arrived late for class that day with the excuse, my teacher looked at me as if I had said my dog ate my homework.

Money was tight while I was in college. Every morning before the start of my hectic day, I would tell myself it would all be worth it when I got my degree and was able to support my family. There were times when I seriously considered dropping out of school because it was too hard to deal with everything. I couldn't have made it without the support of my family. I lived at home with my dad, and he helped me out financially. My mom and friends watched James sometimes too, so I could study. But it was my attention James always craved. He did not understand that I had a final the next day and I needed to study.

Jessica Coombe is a mother who recognized that struggling for a few years is better than struggling for the rest of her life.

Professor, May I Bring My Baby to Class?

Or that I was too exhausted to keep my eyes open and needed to go to bed. He just wanted to play with his mom.

I learned it is better to just go to school than to struggle through life wondering what could have been.

Now a college graduate, I have accomplished my goal. I learned it is better to just go to school than to struggle through life wondering what could have been. I plan to continue my education in the near future.

Jessica Coombe grew up in two households in Pennsylvania, sharing herself with both her parents. She enjoys spending time with her son while working as an x-ray technician. Jessica is a 2006 graduate of Harcum College.

Meet Desiree

I never really had a desire to pursue a college education. I saw all my friends apply to colleges and universities but did not think that was an option for me. Initially, it was the fear of failure that held me back—fear of not succeeding, not meeting everyone else's expectations. The thought of going to school for four more years brought back bad memories. Four more years sounded like a long time.

Even if I did go back, what degree would I pursue? My grandmother wanted me to be a nurse. She knew that I loved helping people, and that was her dream as well. Once I realized that I did not like the sight of blood, I knew that we both were wrong. I was unsure what I wanted to do. All I knew was that I wanted to make a difference—help people and be an inspiration for others.

When I was in my senior year in high school, I found myself in a situation that seemed grim. I was pregnant with my first daughter. I was determined not to drop out of high school or have to go to summer or night school. I went to school every day until my baby was born. With the help of my friends, I did my schoolwork from

Desiree LaMarr is a mother who persevered for fourteen years to earn her degree while raising five daughters.

home and turned it all in when I returned to school six weeks after Briannah was born. Although I had people willing to help me, I knew that it was my responsibility so I found a sitter and dropped Briannah off at a day care across the street from my school and continued on to class.

That year I graduated with the rest of my class. It was a challenge, but I did it. In May, I met the man who would later become my husband, Christopher. Although he was not my child's father, he never treated her any differently. His friends teased him at times for continuing a serious relationship, but he loved both of us enough to stay around.

That fall I entered Community College of Philadelphia. It was the scariest thing that I had ever done. I saw myself as a fish out of water, but I knew I had to continue. I couldn't let my grandmother down. She was my pride and joy, and I was hers too. She told me that she would take care of Briannah during the week so long as I finished school. She would pick Briannah up on Sunday nights, and I would visit them during the week, and then bring Briannah home on Fridays. This continued as I worked and went to college for three years.

Then one of the most devastating events of my life happened. Early one Sunday morning, my grandmother called me to tell me that my grandfather was sick, and she needed me to bring him some soup. I did not want her to know that I was sick too. Christopher and I had recently moved in together, and I was pregnant with Imani, daughter number two. Later, I got a call that I needed to go to the hospital right away. I drove as fast as I could, but when I got there, I was informed that my grandmother had a stroke that morning. I remember walking into her room and realizing that my life would never be the same again. This was in February, just days before my twenty-first birthday. She was declared brain dead and was given only a short time to live. I was devastated. What would I do? She was my whole world. Just then I realized that I was all grown up and that I needed to handle my business. I found a wonderful day care for Briannah and Imani when she was born, nine days before my grandmother passed away. I dropped out of school and worked full time to support my family.

The following year, Christopher and I married. In that same year Nia, girl number three was born, and I returned to college and worked full time. Then in 2004, girl number four, Janae, was born. That was a hard year. My marriage was in serious trouble, and a fire had destroyed everything I owned just the previous year, but I was determined that I would honor my grandmother's memory and finish school. My husband and I separated that year, and I once again became a single mother, now of four daughters. There is nothing more discouraging than to feel that I was not only a failure as a student but as a wife and mother as well. I dropped out of school again and worked like a slave to support my children. I moved around a lot and was unsure of what path I should take.

Then I realized that I needed to stop feeling sorry for myself and get my degree. Two friends that I met through my job were in college and working too. They encouraged me to keep going. My husband and I went to counseling and tried to work through some difficult areas in our relationship. Then, you guessed it, here comes Camille, baby number five. I heard my grandmother saying, "You'll keep getting what you been getting if you keep doin' what you been doin'." So this time I didn't drop out of school.

Then I realized that I needed to stop feeling sorry for myself and get my degree.

In January 2005 I was laid off my job, but praise be to God, in May 2006 I graduated from Community College of Philadelphia with my associate degree in elementary education. Some may say that it took me eleven years to do what I should have been able to do in two years, but for some people it takes a little longer.

The story doesn't end there because in 2007, at thirty years old, I entered Temple University in pursuit of my bachelor's degree in elementary special education, and I will graduate in 2009. I don't plan to stop there. If given the opportunity, I will keep climbing higher and higher until I get my master's degree. In all that I have been through, God has allowed all types of stumbling blocks and pitfalls to come my way, but I can say without a shadow of a doubt that I am stronger today than I have ever been, and even if I don't go any further, I know that I came a lot further than a lot of people said I would. So, to all those women who say "I can't, I won't"—if you have even a mustard seed of faith and give a little effort, you can do anything.

Desiree LaMarr lives in Philadelphia, Pennsylvania, with her five daughters. She earned an associate degree in 2006 from Community College of Philadelphia. She is currently working toward earning her bachelor's degree in elementary education from Temple University where she expects to graduate in December of 2009. Desiree loves life, shopping, and spending time with her family.

Meet Danielle

When I graduated from high school, I had a plan for my future: go to college, meet a wonderful man, graduate, find a great-paying job, get married, have children, and live happily ever after. As you know, life does not always go as planned. Before I knew it, I had dropped out of college, married my high school sweetheart, who had recently joined the army, and moved to Georgia. I now had a new plan. I was twenty years old, living away from home, and I was alone. My husband was sent to war. He came home a few times, and I did what everyone else was doing—had a baby. I tried, over the years, to return to college. I did not like that I depended on my husband for money. I hated having to plead and beg to get a dollar. We had one car, and his work came first. I had to wait.

Years went by, five to be exact, and my life took a turn for the worse. My husband wanted out of our marriage. I was so afraid! In many ways, I was relieved that I no longer had to live with someone who hit me and belittled me. I was twenty-five years old, alone, with no money or education; I had no job or car. What I did have were

Danielle Raitt is a mother who recognized that her only hope for providing for her children was to get an education.

Professor, May I Bring My Baby to Class?

two healthy, beautiful children and my pride. My son was three years old, and my daughter, a newborn. Not at all part of my plan, not even close.

I was very fortunate to have a supportive mother who allowed me and the children to move back home. I somehow managed to get up every morning. I know now it was because of my children. I found a job in a local Head Start classroom. I bought a beat-up car. I rented a small apartment. I met wonderful and supportive people. I slowly crept away from my sorrow. One day, I decided that I would go back to school.

I wondered how I would manage to work a forty-hour workweek, attend college, and be a mom. It seemed impossible, but there had to be a way. I began researching colleges and spent some time contemplating what type of work I wanted to do. I knew that I needed to find a job that would support my family and at the same time that I would enjoy.

Soon the day arrived. Eight years later, I found myself standing in my cap and gown, waiting for the moment to march in and receive my degree. I did it!

I enrolled in school and attended classes in the evening. I started feeling empowered. I'm doing it, I would say to myself. I want to help other single mothers go back to school. I applied for financial aid and was awarded a full Pell Grant. I also took out student loans to pay for what the grants did not cover, as well as to purchase a computer for my home.

It was hard, but I was doing it. I would work all day, drop off the children at my mother's house, and then go to school in the evening. I found ways to sneak in study time. I still remember sitting on the bathroom floor while the kids took a bath, studying for a geology test. Those are good memories—even the wet term paper. At times I thought I could not handle another research project. I felt discouraged and very tired. Sometimes I would take a term off to rest. I knew my limits, and as much as I wanted to finish as quickly as possible, I knew sometimes a breather was necessary.

Soon the day arrived. Eight years later, I found myself standing in my cap and gown, waiting for the moment to march in and receive my degree. I did it! I marched with so much pride I thought I would burst. As my children watched, I thought of the conversation I had had with my daughter earlier that morning. She told me she could not wait until it was her turn to graduate from college. I realized at that point that my hard work resulted not only in a degree but the future of my daughter's education.

Danielle Raitt resides in North Waterboro, Maine, with her three children, Aidan, Sara, and Jacob, and her significant other. Danielle returned to college after a ten year absence from school to complete her bachelor's degree from Franklin Pierce College (now University) in 2006. She enjoys singing in a local community chorale as well as spending time with family.

3

What Can I Do about Child Care?

One of the biggest obstacles facing young mothers who are in school is child care. Who's going to watch your children while you're in school, and how are you going to pay for their care?

A few years ago, I asked Yodeski, a young mother attending Villanova University in Pennsylvania, who was watching her child while she was in school. She said her roommate and friends took turns watching her infant while she attended classes. Otherwise, she took her baby to class with her. Yodeski, a young mother from Rhode Island, was finishing her senior year of college when she had her baby. With no family nearby, no dependable child care, and no money to pay for child care, she had a big problem. However, Yodeski was determined to finish school. She would be the first in her family to get a college degree. Fortunately, since she had only a few months of school left before graduating, Yodeski's concerns about having child care while in school would be short-lived.

Yodeski is not the first student to take her child to class. Many students, if the professor allows, take their children to class when their regular child care arrangements fall through. But not all professors are sympathetic to a student-parent's situation. Many, and rightfully so, will conclude that it's not fair to the other students to have a child in the classroom who might disrupt the lesson.

The organization I started in 1998, Family Care Solutions, Inc. (FCS), helps low-income single mothers pay for child care while they

Success is to be measured not so much by the position that one has reached in life, as by the obstacles which he has overcome while trying to succeed.

Booker T. Washington

pursue their dream of earning a college degree. Just like you, they are strong, courageous, bold, and intelligent. FCS awarded Yodeski a child care scholarship to a licensed, quality child care center where loving, dependable, and nurturing people cared for her baby. If you're in a situation where you are asking someone to watch your child from day-to-day or week-to-week, you should find dependable child care. Enrolling your child in a licensed child care program ensures that someone is always there to take care of your child.

Describe your experience of taking your child to class or a school activity:

Keeping it REAL

_____

_____

_____

_____

_____

_____

CHOOSING QUALITY CHILD CARE

Back in the day, it was nice to have grandma take care of my son whenever I couldn't. I trusted her, knowing that she would love him all day long—hold him, kiss him, sing to him, talk to him, and nurture him. He would get all of her attention. But as he got older, I realized he needed to interact with other kids his age. Being at grandma's house all day, every day, became restrictive. He needed others who would stimulate and challenge his curious little mind. He needed to have the freedom to play in open areas. He needed to be in an environment that would meet his needs socially and academically. I chose to put my son in an early childhood education program. It was the best decision for both of us. He enjoyed learning and playing with other kids. I was happy too, after I got through the separation anxiety.

Many child care facilities have professional care providers who will nurture and love your child almost as much as you. (I say almost, because no one can love your child more than you do.) Children begin learning very early in life. It's important that their developmental and social needs are met when they are young. Those who participate in an early childhood education program are better prepared for kindergarten.[1]

When choosing a child care facility, start by ensuring the facility is licensed to operate. A licensed child care provider is monitored by your local government. To become licensed, a provider must meet state and city regulations and training requirements. You may choose from a home-based or center-based facility. Home-based child care, or family child care, is provided in the caregiver's home, not yours. Center-based care is provided in a facility specifically used to care for a large group of children and is not in a person's home.[2]

A home- or center-based facility may participate in programs that help it improve the quality of care given to children. An accredited facility or a facility participating in a quality rating program is regulated by government or private agencies to measure the facility's progress on improving the quality of care. Accreditation means that the child care program has completed a set of requirements established by a nationally recognized organization or by your local government.[3] The National Association for the Education of Young Children (NAEYC) is the most recognized accrediting agency in the country, but it's not the only one. Providers who offer child care in their homes may be accredited by the National Association of Family Child Care (NAFCC). See appendix A for how to find more information about these organizations and others.

Earning accreditation is based on a set of requirements and standards established by a group of experts in the field of early childhood education. The staff at a facility that is accredited has made a commitment to improve the quality of care to ensure young children are prepared for kindergarten by meeting their developmental and social needs early in life.

To meet these requirements the staff has made these commitments:

▶ Participate in ongoing child development training

▶ Invest in age-appropriate learning materials

▶ Improve its facility by making renovations to comply with health and safety standards.[4]

In other words, an accredited child care program is an age-appropriate environment for young children where staff are specialists in teaching, caring for, and nurturing children. These accredited programs are in place to help you identify and choose quality child care programs. Ask the director at the facility you are considering taking your child to if it is participating in state or city initiatives to improve its services.[5] You may also check your state's child care Web site to find out about quality rating programs that are designed to engage child care providers in the process of improving early childhood education.

Child care providers volunteer to participate in the accreditation process. Only a small percentage of child care providers nationally are accredited.[6] It can cost a lot of money for some providers and take up to a few years to become accredited. So don't be surprised if there are few accredited providers in your neighborhood. Licensed providers who are not accredited offer quality early child care programs too. You may find that staff members working at nonaccredited but licensed facilities have degrees or certificates in early childhood education and receive child care training. For some reason the facility has chosen not to pursue accreditation. Your selection should not be based solely on accreditation, but on the quality of care and age-appropriate learning.

Your goal is to ensure your child will be in a safe, clean, healthy, and loving environment that offers social learning through play and age-appropriate activities. Talk with the director about the facility's policies, programs, and costs. But most importantly, observe and listen to yourself. How do you feel about the child care facility? What was your first reaction? See appendix B for a checklist—"Is This the Right Place for My Child? 38 Research-Based Indicators of High-Quality Child Care" published by the National Association of Child Care Resource and Referral Agencies.[7] Use this checklist as a guide to help you recognize quality child care. Also listed in appendix A are Web sites to help you find quality child care programs in your neighborhood and learn more about quality care and quality rating systems.

When choosing a child care provider, make arrangements as early as possible. Call the facility months before you start school to secure a spot for your child. August and September seem to be the busiest months for providers. Summer camp has ended, families are returning from vacation, and parents are preparing children for a new school year. Child care facilities fill up fast in September. If you wait until you register for classes, the facility may be full. Some have waiting lists that last for months or even a couple of years. Have a backup plan ready just in case your first choice doesn't work out.

Does a relative or friend care for your child while you're in school? Explain why you chose this type of care.

Keeping it
REAL

_____

_____

_____

_____

What type of child care facility (center or home) do you prefer and why?

_____

_____

_____

_____

_____

_____

Are you satisfied with the quality of care your child receives? Explain.

_____

_____

_____

_____

_____

What positive changes have you noticed in your child since starting the child care program?

_____

_____

_____

_____

_____

What negative changes have you noticed in your child since starting the child care program?

_____

_____

_____

_____

_____

Have you talked with the provider about your observations? Describe the discussion.

_____

_____

_____

_____

_____

PAYING FOR CHILD CARE

Of the many factors that affect your decision to go to college, tuition is probably the biggest, but child care can be a major determining factor. The cost of child care varies depending on where you live, the age of your child, the type of facility (home or center), staff credentials, and accreditation. Child care can cost more than tuition at your local community college. The average cost to attend a public community college in 2008 was $2,361 during the academic year.[8] What is the cost of full-time child care for your young child during the academic year?

Although there is help to pay for college, there's little help to pay for child care while you go to college. As mentioned earlier, over seventeen hundred child care centers have been established on college campuses. Some offer child care services based on a sliding-fee scale or provide student-parent discounts. Payment using the sliding-fee scale is based on your income. Some on-campus facilities may also award child care stipends or scholarships. See the previous chapter and appendix A to learn how to identify colleges with on-campus child care centers that offer financial assistance.

Your neighborhood child care facilities may also offer child care scholarships, two-for-one grants for twins, or sibling discounts. Call child care providers in your community and ask if they offer assistance to help low-income parents who are going to college. You may hear a care provider say, "I was a single mother going to college too. Sure, I'll help you." Check your local YMCA, Boys and Girls Club, community child care networks, and other organizations that offer child care and after-school programs.

Here are a few government assistance programs to help you pay for child care.

Temporary Assistance for Needy Families (TANF) This federal program, often referred to as welfare, is designed to help people transition from unemployment to employment. The idea is to get all parents who are able to work into employment so they can work to become economically self-sufficient and independent of government assistance. Depending on where you live and your circumstance you may be required to work twenty or more hours per week, with the exception of teen parents. For those in college, some states allow study hours, as well as work study, to be combined with class hours to fulfill the work requirement. Recent changes in TANF rules allow recipients to go to college full time for twelve months as a federally countable work activity. TANF recipients have this twelve-month opportunity to concentrate primarily on their studies while pursuing their associate, bachelor's, or advanced degree. This is particularly helpful for those who only need a few credits to earn their degree. In most states, after twelve months, recipients are required to participate in other work activities for at least twenty hours per week while they continue to go to school.[10] Depending on your state rules, TANF recipients may be eligible for financial assistance and special allowances to help with these expenses:

- Child care
- Books and supplies
- Clothing and uniforms
- Equipment and tools
- Education and training fees

- Private and public transportation
- Other financial assistance as needed to participate in the program, such as eyeglasses and hearing aids[11]

Additionally, recipients could be eligible for housing allowances, medical assistance, and food stamps.[12] Support services vary from state to state depending on your income. Even if you're not receiving cash assistance through TANF, you may still be eligible for child care subsidies. Call your local public assistance agency to see if you qualify for any of these services.

Head Start This federally sponsored program is free for qualified low-income families with children from birth to age five. It promotes growth and development and school readiness for young children.[13]

Child Care Access Means Parents in School (CCAMPIS) This federal grant program helps colleges and universities assist low-income student-parents with child care costs. CCAMPIS funds help male and female students pay for child care, before- and after-school care, evening care, or weekend care.[14]

Local Programs Your local child care resource and referral agency offers state or county-funded child care subsidies, stipends, or vouchers. Subsidies may be based on your income, work hours, or school hours.[15]

See appendix A for Web sites of organizations to help you pay for child care.

What type of financial support do you have to help pay for child care?

_____

_____

_____

Keeping it REAL

List the people who care for your child when he or she is not in a child care program (for example, in the evenings and on weekends):

_____

_____

_____

_____

SEPARATION ANXIETY

For most moms, including me, that first day at day care is harder for the mother than the child. I was a nervous wreck all day. I couldn't concentrate on anything. I called the provider to check on my son a few times that day. I was a mess. But my son loved it. Playing with the other kids and sharing toys—he was in his zone. He didn't even cry when I dropped him off the next morning. He just waved his hand and said good-bye with a smile on his face. However, I didn't keep bringing him back there for very long. I went to pick him up a few times near closing time and saw him playing on the indoor jungle gym, alone. Someone was supposed to be watching my baby! I eventually pulled him out and enrolled him in a great program. Never settle for less than what you expect. You always have a choice. And when it comes to your child, choose the best.

Before enrolling your child in day care for the first time, consider a trial run for a day or two. Take part in the activities or sit quietly as your child explores her new surroundings. Talk to her about leaving, always telling her that you will return later to pick her up. Your child care provider may have other suggestions on how you and your child can overcome separation anxiety. The provider should be willing to provide daily reports of your child's activities and progress, at least until you and she become comfortable with her new environment.

How did you prepare your child for the first day at the child care facility?

Keeping it REAL

_____

_____

_____

_____

_____

_____

_____

Were you more anxious about starting a new child care program than your child was? Explain.

_____

_____

_____

_____

_____

How did your child react when you picked him or her up?

_____

_____

_____

_____

_____

What do you like about the child care facility?

_____

_____

_____

_____

_____

_____

Professor, May I Bring My Baby to Class?

Are you ready to take action? Read these real-life stories of mothers who were challenged by the lack of child care and other related issues. Learn how they accessed community and public assistance to keep them on the road to earning their degrees. Family support was also instrumental in helping these moms through difficult times.

Meet De'Asia

It hasn't been easy, but I feel it has been totally worth it. I gave birth to my daughter Arica in my sophomore year at The Ohio State University.

After having Arica, I made it a goal to finish school on time—within four years as initially planned. I took off the quarter when Arica was due. She was born in December. I returned to school in the spring without her. That was one of the hardest times I ever endured. She was only three months old when I left her at home in Cleveland. I feel I missed out on a lot. I would go home every weekend to see her and make sure she didn't forget about me. I wanted so badly for her to be with me at Ohio State. I began to seek out help to see if I could bring Arica to live with me on campus. Ohio State has a program that supports single parents. With the help of the ACCESS Collaborative Program through the Office of Minority Affairs, I was able to get Arica into the on-campus child care center, which normally has a wait list of almost two years. The next step was finding an apartment. After having made preparations for Arica to join me at school, I returned the following fall. I was so happy.

I made sure my professors were aware of my situation. Surprisingly, they were very understanding. If there was anything I had trouble with, they would help. One day, when I was late dropping my daughter off at the day care center, I ran into one of my professors whose class I was supposed to be in. He was totally understanding because he was going through the same thing. I've even had to take

De'Asia Davis is a mother who advocated bringing her daughter to school with her.

Arica to class with me. She got sick at day care, and they sent her home. She couldn't return for twenty-four hours, and I had class the next day, so I e-mailed my instructor to see if I could bring her. She said it was okay; the class loved having her. I asked if she was too much trouble because I thought maybe she was too giggly or something, but the instructor said she could come to class anytime. It really took a load off me to know that it was okay for her to be there if I needed to bring her.

One thing I've learned since having Arica is that life doesn't stop because you are in school. Arica wasn't planned, but my life had to go on. I am determined to make a good life for her, and it is totally possible. I have a wonderful support system. My mother and friends help me out tremendously. I've had to take Saturday classes, work, and go to meetings, and they are there to help me out. I didn't dwell on having a child in school because sometimes it can become a crutch. I made sure I got my work in on time; I had to put in more effort because the luxury of studying whenever I wanted to was gone. I always did my best. I have kept my grades up and remained on the dean's list since having Arica.

> *One thing I've learned since having Arica is that life doesn't stop because you are in school.*

I want the very best for my daughter. I know that an education is going to allow me to give her all she needs. I don't want her to be a statistic because she happens to come from a single-parent home. I want her to be an outlier. I don't want to be a statistical "baby mama" because that's what society expects. She has given me the boost that I needed to go on and do big things.

De'Asia Davis graduated from The Ohio State University with a bachelor's degree in sociology in June 2008. She plans to continue her education in the fall of 2009 in pursuit of a master's degree in social work. De'Asia aspires to become a lawyer to practice child advocacy and family law. She enjoys shopping, photography, and relaxing with family and friends.

Meet Catella

In my sophomore year at Temple University, I found out I was pregnant. I thought my life was over. I did not know what to do. Everyone around me told me to have an abortion, but that was not an option. My partner was okay at first, even excited, until he told his overpowering family; they told him to forget about a baby and to follow his plans for his future. They told him I just wanted to trap him because he was a good man in college—like I wasn't a good woman in college. Needless to say, he listened and left. Within a few months of the pregnancy, I was by myself. My family lived over three hours away. I had two roommates who were not ideal role models for my baby—they drank and (like typical college kids) partied at night—so I had to move, which meant my rent would increase. Being a full-time student, I didn't work. I applied for welfare assistance and grants and took out student loans to help with expenses. The loans paid for my apartment, and welfare paid for my medical and food expenses.

I never missed a beat. The semester I was due, I took one weekend class on campus and three on-line classes from home. I finished the semester with decent grades. I had an amazing, beautiful baby girl, Azarea. She weighed 7.77 pounds. My mother, grandmother, and sister were with me when my daughter was born. My sister was able to stay with me for a while to help out.

I got an apartment in North Philly for $600 a month. It became unbearable to live there. The neighborhood kids harassed my sister, I caught a roach crawling in Azarea's crib from the dirty neighbors next door, and to top it off, my apartment was broken into. What little I had was stolen. Needless to say, I had to move again. My family helped me get a better apartment.

When it was time to go back to school, I was unable to find reliable child care. So I ended up taking Azarea to class with me until my professors asked me to stop. So here I am, missing class, at the grocery store, upset because I don't have anyone to watch

Catella Visser is a mother who entrusted her daughter to a woman she barely knew when she was unable to find affordable child care.

my daughter, when I meet a woman in the parking lot. I asked her, because she had children with her, if she knew of affordable child care, and conveniently, she pulled out child-abuse clearances, first-aid cards, her ID, etc. (She is a foster parent—that is why she had all that information.) Her name is Tia, and she said she could watch Azarea, and not only that, she would come to my apartment so the baby could stay in her own surroundings! I was so excited. God was looking out for me; He came through with a solution. So the next day I made it to my classes. I was so nervous, I must have called Tia a million times. I was stressed; I left my baby alone, in my apartment, with a woman I barely knew. I started to panic. I left after my second class and ran home to check on her. Everything was fine. The next day I made it through my classes.

> *I wanted to give her the world, and I worked hard, managed my time between schoolwork, and spent as much time as possible with her.*

I started working at night at a local bar making pretty good money and working during the day at Temple between classes. Tia and I became very good friends. It was nice to have someone with children who was not about going out and partying like my other "friends," who all seemed to disappear after my daughter was born. I felt very alone. At night I would do my schoolwork and cuddle with my daughter. She instantly became my world. Nothing else mattered. I started to excel in school, and I wanted to be something great for her, someone she would look up to. I wanted to give her the world, and I worked hard, managed my time between schoolwork, and spent as much time as possible with her.

I graduated on time with a bachelor's degree in sociology. Being in school was beneficial for my daughter. I worked with her all the time. I would read my schoolbooks to her and study my Spanish with her. Her vocabulary is immaculate for a four-year-old. She is the smartest kid in her class.

Professor, May I Bring My Baby to Class?

My daughter changed my life and made me the woman I am today. I would not change a thing, and doing it alone made our relationship very special.

Catella Visser graduated Temple University in 2005 with a bachelor's degree in sociology. She is currently attending Delaware Technical & Community College to become a registered nurse. Catella works as a case manager for the mentally ill population. She owns her own house in New Castle, Delaware. Azarea has started kindergarten and was accepted into a special "gifted" program.

Meet**Kendra**

I made a decision early on not to let my dreams of attending college die after confirmation of my pregnancy two months before my high school graduation. Instead of entering Rutgers University as an excited freshman during the fall semester of 1988, I entered the realm of motherhood.

Kendra Newman is a mother who used public assistance as a temporary hand up as she worked to earn a degree in telecommunications.

Canceling my engagement to my son's father was very wise. No one deserves to be abused, and staying would have set a horrible example for our child and probably cost one of us our lives or freedom. Choosing to attend a technical institute offered distance from the jealous rages and a baccalaureate degree with intense hands-on experience that equipped me to compete in the surging technology wave of the 1990s.

Being a young, single mother has universal challenges. Add to them my mother's diagnosis of lung cancer, an unenforced child-support order, and the need to work two jobs to make ends meet; my grades began to nosedive. Eventually, I was placed on academic probation. Feeling defeated, I had a good cry and took a year off to regroup and construct a plan B.

Easing back into school by taking a limited number of classes to allow me to spend more time with my son and parents put many miles on the car they gave me, but I'm so glad I did. I had no idea that my mom—my best friend, biggest supporter, and cheerleader—would succumb to her illness so soon. My mother's death forced me into full responsibility as a mother. Without her coparenting I was solely responsible for child care, healthcare, and the total well-being of my three-year-old. I was always behind in day care tuition, and it was impossible to pay for vaccinations and the countless doctor visits necessary for toddlers.

Reluctantly, I had to turn to public assistance. At first I was ashamed. Later I began to see it for what it should be—a temporary hand up. My year as a welfare recipient afforded me the ability to concentrate on being the best mom I could be and reduced my son's time in day care from eleven hours to four hours per day. We received adequate healthcare at no charge and much more.

This journey has required of me resilience and tenacity. I refused to settle for an associate degree as many had suggested and pressed on toward my bachelor of science, which required me to relocate to the midwest. Moving to Illinois was a stressful time—so many miles from home, knowing almost no one, strapped financially, and being home bound because of severe weather would be enough to force many to call it quits. I stuck it out and relied on God to provide for all of my needs. Spending quality time with my son, going to bed at 8:00 p.m. when he did, then rising at 2:00 a.m. to study and complete assignments was the perfect formula for earning a 3.4 GPA my senior year.

> *This journey has required of me resilience and tenacity. I refused to settle for an associate degree as many had suggested and pressed on toward my bachelor of science, which required me to relocate to the midwest.*

I spent countless weekends in the public library with my son. He thought it was fun, and it was free! There I became reacquainted with the writing of Maya Angelou, reading everything she had written, from her autobiographical story, *I Know Why the Caged Bird Sings*, to *All God's*

Children Need Traveling Shoes and every bit of her poetry in between. Her honest recollection of her life as a young, single mom gave me the fuel I needed to know that someone had already been through and not only survived but succeeded in what I was yet to encounter.

On June 18, 1994, I walked across the stage in Wheaton, Illinois, to receive my diploma. My father and other family members had flown in to celebrate with me. The most important person in the audience that day was my five-year-old son, who had "attended" college before he'd ever stepped foot into a kindergarten classroom.

To young parents pursuing goals of higher education, I want to say that the years of pain, sweat, and tears are well worth it. Holding a degree has been my ticket to compete in a financial arena that would otherwise be off limits. Education gives us choices and affords us the opportunity to choose where we live, work, and send our children to school.

Find a good mentor; look for someone who has already been where you're going and ask for constructive criticism. Educate yourself regarding finances. Once you've set yourself up for great earning potential, let the days of not having enough be a distant memory.

Adversity can be used to propel you to new heights. I know now that the culmination of my experiences have tested and built my strengths and taught hard lessons, but I've made it through and will look to these life events to encourage myself and others when problems arise.

Lastly, I encourage you to tell your story! Others need to know that the obstacles they are facing can be conquered.

Kendra Newman is the director of information technology for the College of Health Professions at Temple University in Philadelphia, Pennsylvania. She holds a bachelor's degree in telecommunications management from DeVry Institute of Technology, a master's degree in project management from Keller Graduate School, and she has earned the well-regarded project management professional (PMP) credential from the Project Management Institute. Her son, Darren, will begin his junior year at Temple University in the fall of 2009.

Meet**Dawn**

I am writing this story hoping to inspire at least one mother who may think it is impossible to pursue her dream of going to college, while facing the challenge of being a single mother. I am a thirty-six year old mother of four children. When I graduated from high school in 1990, I thought I had my life planned out. I attended Gordon Phillips Beauty School, graduated, received my cosmetology license, and started working in a hair salon. Life seemed okay. I met a guy who I thought was a good person. We bought a house together and decided to start a family. The father of my children ended up being a liar, thief, and heroin addict. I had family that would have helped me in a minute. I was too proud. I kept my problems to myself. When there was no food, I went to food banks. At Christmas time I signed up for programs that gave me toys to give my kids. I was ashamed to have picked such a horrible person to be the father of my kids. I did not want my kids to suffer so I did what I could to give them a normal childhood.

As time went on, I started thinking about how I really wanted to be a nurse. I wanted to make something of myself that would set a good example for my kids and give my family financial stability. The question that kept coming to mind was, How could I do this? How could I be a full-time mom and still go to college? The most important issue was my son, who was three years old when I enrolled. He wasn't in school yet, and I could not afford child care. I decided to try it anyway and enrolled at Community College of Philadelphia. I learned about the greatest program, Child Care Access Means Parents in School. The program paid for my son's day care, which allowed me to attend college. I don't have to worry about child care payments since the program pays for the child care as long as I follow the program rules. Things have been going well. I have almost completed all the prerequisites that I need to apply to the nursing program. I am maintaining a B average. I am not going to lie and say this is easy;

Dawn Gallagher-Gonzalez is a mother who took advantage of community and government assistance.

Professor, May I Bring My Baby to Class?

it's not, but I am proud of myself and my children are proud of their mom. I hope this inspires anyone who thought it couldn't be done. If I can do this, so can you. God bless you and good luck.

Dawn Gallagher-Gonzalez lives in Philadelphia, Pennsylvania, with her four children; a fifteen-year-old, eleven-year-old twins, and a four-year-old. She completed the prerequisite courses necessary for entrance into a nursing school in December 2008 at Community College of Philadelphia. She is currently waiting to hear of her acceptance into a nursing program in the Philadelphia region. Dawn enjoys spending time with her family.

Meet**Kameela**

My mom always instilled in me the power of education and the importance of school. So when I got pregnant in my senior year of high school and gave birth to my son, Kameron, I did not let that deter me from going to college. After graduation, I attended my neighborhood community college, Cosumnes River College. At times I had to bring my son to class with me because I did not have a regular sitter during the day to watch him. This was very stressful. Along with my rigorous schoolwork load, I was a new single mother, a full-time student, and I worked part time. However, with prayer and loving support from my family, I was able to cope as a student and parent.

I receive financial aid to help with school expenses and government assistance for necessities like food and diapers through WIC. I am not an advocate for living off public assistance, but I do advocate asking for help when you need it and accepting it as you continue to grow academically and financially through life. It is no piece of cake to be a new mother while working and going to school. It is not a fashion trend nor is it cute; it is definitely a challenge.

After a while, the challenge of trying to keep up with going to school, studying, and working while coping with the pressures of

Kameela Howard is a mother who was challenged at every turn, took a break from school to refocus, and started back when the time was right.

being a new mom caught up with me. I was placed on academic probation because I was unable to maintain passing grades. I somehow thought I was super woman, or should I say super mom. After a trying fall semester at school, I took off the spring semester so I focused solely on Kameron. I continued to work part time. This was hard to do because school has always been a priority in my life. But when you become a mother your child becomes your number-one priority, so you need to do what is best for your child.

My break from school did not last long. My son is now fourteen months old, and I am back in school as a full-time student. I still work too. Kameron is also in day care so it gives me the time I need to study and do my homework. I communicate with my teachers to let them know that I am also a parent. They are understanding and willing to work with me and support my academic endeavors.

Kameron is my motivator. He empowers me to continue setting and reaching my goals. A degree is important to me.

Education, for me, has been my guiding light to success, and I would like to present that light to the world when I become a teacher.

Ever since I was nine years old, I have wanted to go to college. I plan to continue my education in pursuit of a master's degree. Education, for me, has been my guiding light to success, and I would like to present that light to the world when I become a teacher. So failure, for me, is not an option.

Kameela Howard lives in Elkgrove, California, with her son, Kameron. Kameela expects to graduate from Cosumnes River College in the spring of 2010. When not busy with school, she enjoys spending time with family and friends, but over everyone else, her heart and time belong to Kameron.

Meet**Sara**

I am going to be a mother. If that wasn't one of the scariest thoughts I had ever experienced, I don't know what was. I was sixteen, had just finished my sophomore year in high school, and the world was at my fingertips. Disoriented and confused, I found myself in unfamiliar territory. I had plans and dreams, and now, I was scared. I wanted to buy a car, hang out with friends, go to football games, but I knew that the circumstances had changed and that would not be my life. A new responsibility arose and despite my apprehensions, I tried to think positively.

For lack of a better phrase, life was hard. The most struggling aspect of my life became school. I found it extremely hard to concentrate on my homework when I had to deal with the baby always crying, always hungry, and always needing to be changed. The few hours I had to myself after putting the baby to sleep for the night consisted of house chores and more schoolwork. I could not afford child care while I was in school so I went to a special school called the Family Center. The school hours there were similar to "normal" school hours and the schoolwork was just as challenging, but unlike "normal" school, I could bring my son because they offered child care. This allowed me to finish my high school education. The Family Center also taught me about life as a young mother and improved my skills on parenting. They provided a great support team and people that I could talk to about my fears about parenting or just life in general. It was one of the most beneficial places I have ever been.

Life was a struggle during this time. I went to school during the day, worked in the evenings, and then retreated back home for more school. My education had always been important to me, and I worked very hard to get good grades. There were many nights that I felt completely mentally drained. There were times I felt my brain could just not think anymore. I was worried about school, work, bills, my son, and sometimes all at once. I was exhausted. I would

Sara Rulle is a mother who attended a high school that allowed her to bring her son with her to school.

remind myself frequently that on some level or another, I chose this life. I made the choice to have my son. I made the choice to continue my education. I made the choice to work. This life I had created was stressful and difficult, but I also made the choice to never give up. Finally, my hard work had paid off. I received my high school diploma a semester early. This was a great feeling. Finally, I was done!

Wrong! The last thing I want in life is to end up broke, on welfare, with four kids, and no man. I had my high school diploma, which was great, but what type of job could I get with it? I knew I needed to further my education. I also knew that I did not want to become just another statistic. Some people use children as an excuse not to work or go to school. I am not one of them. I want to be a productive member of society. Going to school is a very achievable goal, even for a mother.

I attended my local community college and explored a couple of fields of interest. It took me three years, but I finally received my associate degree. I will not say that it was easy—in fact, it was probably one of the hardest things that I have ever done. Being a single mom and juggling work, school, and a child is a tremendous responsibility. There were many nights where I only had two or three hours of sleep. Whenever I wasn't working, I was either doing schoolwork or taking care of my son. There was no free time. I felt so overwhelmed at times, like the world was just crumbling underneath me. There were nights that I just cried myself to sleep, not wanting to wake up because then I would have to, once again, endure this struggle of a life. There were times I felt broken down and times I felt like quitting.

I never quit. I didn't quit because I wasn't satisfied yet. I was not okay with making minimum wage. I was not okay with my son crying because he was hungry. I was not okay with this poverty-stricken lifestyle! I wanted so much more for us. We deserved better, and I could only rely on myself to get us there.

I currently attend University of Maryland University College, which is close to where I live. I am working on my bachelor's degree in accounting and finance. Times are still hard. They don't get easier as time passes. What I have learned is to not lose sight of your focus point. Keep your goals attainable and take it one step at a time. Pride yourself on what you have already accomplished. I try not to put myself down because I am doing the best that I can do, and that is enough. Keep the people that support you closest to you. These are the people that will encourage you the most and help keep you on your track to success. There will always be people out there that doubt you and think that you are incapable. Let those people go. You don't need them in your life. My son has influenced my life tremendously, even with school. He is my strength. He depends on me, and I know that someday, my degree will be complete, and I can provide for him the way he deserves. I could never look down at his smiling face with those bright blue eyes and tell him that this is as good as it gets. It can be better, and it will be better. Education is my chosen path for success. Even through all of my trials and tribulations, it will be worth it.

> *I have always been one to agree that the hardest moments in life are the ones that make us stronger.*

I have always been one to agree that the hardest moments in life are the ones that make us stronger. In any given situation, the determination, the persistence, and the passion we possess allows us to rise above the rest and shine in our own light. Throughout my life, I have learned that it is not what we say that counts; it is what we do. Our actions in life may bring unexpected situations. It is how we deal with those situations that allow us to learn and grow.

Sara Rulle currently resides in Hagerstown, Maryland, with her son, Kent. She enjoys outdoor sports such as soccer, baseball, and football and also oil painting, jewelry making, and working out. Sara earned her associate degree from Hagerstown Community College in 2008 and currently attends the University of Maryland University College working toward her bachelor's degree.

Meet**Beverly**

My son, Bo, thought his name was "Hurry, Bo," "Come on, Bo," "We gotta go, Bo!" This is primarily how he was addressed by me when he was between the ages of two and five. At that time I was a nontraditional student beginning college as a full-time student, ten years after graduating from high school. I was also a single mother working two and sometimes three jobs at a time. My primary source of income was working as an instructor at a local dance school teaching classes mostly in the late afternoons and early evenings. Some semesters I arranged my class schedule to accommodate teaching a morning exercise class to make a little extra money, especially for the holidays. I was also a bookkeeper for a locally owned fast-food restaurant and periodically worked as a coat-checker at the country club—anything I could do to bring in more money to help make ends meet.

I vividly remember having to make choices about what I had time for and what could wait. Each day I made a mental list of what needed to be done in my family life, my academic life, and my work life. Shave my legs? Go to the grocery store because we were out of everything? Work on my research paper? Get the paychecks ready for payday? Work on the choreography for a new jazz dance? I found myself wearing mostly slacks to school—especially when finding time for personal hygiene activities was limited!

Without the support of my family, I would never have been able to even consider enrolling in school and completing my degrees. I depended on my parents to provide child care for Bo throughout this period. He was enrolled in a local child care program during the mornings while I was in class. My mother picked him up early each afternoon, took him to her home, fed him supper, and many times he was bathed and ready for bed when I picked him up after teaching dance. My supper was waiting for me when I got there and, some days, also my clean laundry and some needed groceries too.

Beverly Wiginton is a mother who worked hard to make "someday" finally come.

Professor, May I Bring My Baby to Class?

One summer when I was enrolled in an evening class, I remember taking Bo to my parents' home, and my younger sister was there as well. Just before I left, my father, mother, sister, and I were talking on the patio. As we continued talking, without ever interrupting the conversation, one by one, Bo took the hand of my father, my mother, and then my sister, and guided them back toward the house until we were separated by some distance. We did not really notice what was happening until Bo stated, "Now, Mama, you can leave." It was as if he was making sure that if I was not with him, other important people in his life were. The incident was quite profound to me in realizing the relationships he had developed with the important people supporting me in my life.

I applied for a student loan to attend graduate school. I only borrowed enough to pay tuition for two years. I discovered that I could request more than I had originally requested, so I decided to get more and take advantage of the bank's "generosity." That was the year Bo was five and a trip to Disney World in Florida seemed to be important in his life, so with the help of my student loan, it became a reality. It took ten years to pay off the student loan, but it was definitely worth it when I look back at the pictures and recall events from our Disney World adventure.

Just recently, Bo told me how proud he is of where I am and what I am doing for others now.

Many times when shopping, Bo would ask for toys, games, and other items that our budget just would not support. I would answer his request with, "Maybe someday." Just recently, Bo told me how proud he is of where I am and what I am doing for others now. He mentioned some specific instances when money was a real issue for us and said he realized that now we both are in a much better place financially. He said, "I guess 'someday' has finally come!"

Now, as an early childhood educator and director of a campus-based early childhood program, I am sometimes embarrassed and almost ashamed of what I put Bo through during those undergraduate and then graduate school years. Those times were financially, physically, and many times emotionally challenging. Today, he is twenty-eight, a college graduate, a talented musician, and the music department manager of a local Barnes & Noble Booksellers. I completed both my undergraduate and graduate degrees, graduating summa cum laude. I began working for the same university in the campus early childhood program. My first role was head teacher in our brand-new infant-toddler program, and five years later I became director of the program. This year, I am celebrating my twentieth year working in our campus early childhood program.

Would I have changed my circumstances if I could have? If you had asked me this question twenty years ago, I probably would have said, "Absolutely!" But as I look back on those times today, I feel a little flutter and tickle in my heart. It was worth every single struggle, tear, and frustration because the relationship I have with my son, Bo, is very strong and based on supporting one another through those tough years. Yes, "someday" indeed finally comes to all of us!

Beverly Wiginton grew up in Johnson City, Tennessee. She holds a master's degree from East Tennessee State University and is director of the Child Study Center Early Childhood Program. Beverly is married, with one son and four dogs. She enjoys yoga, quilting, knitting, reading, and walking.

CHAPTER 4

How to Become a Successful Student-Parent

Your faith and courage have brought you this far. Now let your determination carry you the rest of the way. Going to college with a child is very different from going to high school with a child. You will have to adjust to a new schedule, learn at a faster pace, and become a responsible adult.

To become a successful student, you will need to be disciplined, organized, and focused. To become a successful student-parent, you will need support from family, friends, your professors, advisors, and a dependable child care provider. Family and friends can help out as you need them. For example, you might need someone to pick up your child from the child care provider so that you can stay late on campus to study with your work group or someone to watch your child so you can take a nap. Get to know your professors early and make sure they know you are a student-parent with the hope that, when an emergency arises, they will be understanding of your needs. Classmates can help out too, for example, by taking notes to share when you are absent. Meeting with your advisors regularly can help you manage your class schedule. Of course, you need reliable child care so you can go to school or work.

Managing your daily activities may be difficult at first, but eventually you and your child will establish a daily routine. Deahna

The greatest barrier to success is the fear of failure.

Sven Goran Eriksson

Byrd and Rachel DeStefanis, students at Community College of Philadelphia, share these helpful tips on becoming a successful student-parent:

- Tour the campus before the first day of classes to learn where your classes are being held.
- Get plenty of rest the night before your first day of classes.
- Prepare your child's clothing and child care needs for the entire week.
- Prepare your child's lunch and snack the night before.
- Prepare your book bag for school and your child's bag for child care the night before.
- Wake up early allowing yourself enough time to eat breakfast with your child.
- Allow yourself enough time to take your baby to the child care provider and get to campus to relax before your first class.
- Check with your child care provider weekly to make sure your child has sufficient supplies, such as diapers, snacks, and a change of clothes.
- Stay on top of your homework.
- Use your time wisely; study as much as you can on campus during breaks and after classes.
- Keep a calendar for due dates and deadlines.
- Keep a copy of the *MLA Handbook for Writers of Research Papers* (published by the Modern Language Association) to help with writing research papers.
- Don't be afraid to ask for help.
- When you're feeling overwhelmed and stressed, take a breather.

A successful student will know her limits. If you need to shift your schedule around to better manage your life, do it. If you need to let go of some activities or people to become more focused, do it. If you need to make adjustments to become more organized, do it. If you need a break, take one. If you need a longer break, take one. Whatever you need to do to stay on track to earning your degree—do it. A successful student will one day say, "I did what I needed to do, and now I have my degree."

How was your first day at college? Was it everything you expected? Explain.

Keeping it
REAL

_____

_____

_____

_____

_____

SCHOOL, WORK, AND A BABY?

How could anyone ever doubt the success of a single mom who goes to college full time, works, and cares for her child? Look at all the skills she possesses. She is a multitasker. She's organized and knows how to prioritize. She meets deadlines and can handle a crisis. She is patient and is a quick learner. She can endure long hours to get the job done. She knows how to budget and gets the most from what she has. She is determined and focused.

For many moms in college, work is not a choice but a necessity. And the situation can become a vicious cycle because her ability to go to school depends on child care, which depends on work, and her ability to work depends on child care.

Some women have managed their financial aid, student loans, and welfare support well enough to take care of themselves and their children without having to work. This allows more time to focus on school and parenting. That extra time studying most likely will boost her grades and will help her graduate sooner rather than later.

How can you go to school, work, and care for your baby? Exercise the Power of You and believe that you can and push past your fears and doubt. Those who are successful at this balancing act have become skillful masters at organizing, scheduling, and student-parenting. These are learned behaviors that you can become proficient at too. Eventually your days will become routine, and your child will learn to follow the daily ritual without much fuss. You will get tired, cry, feel guilty about not spending enough time with your child, and want to quit, but hang in there! Look at those bright eyes, that adorable little face, and those lovable cheeks and remember why you're going through all this in the first place.

To help you stay organized use the Managing My Schedule planner in appendix C. You can create a calendar for each school semester or trimester of important dates—like your doctor's appointments, child's class trip, finals, project and paper due dates, study group sessions, work schedule, or a day at the zoo with the kids. Make a copy and share your schedule with family members who are helping you with your child while you're going to school. You may also build your schedule on-line and print extra copies from our Web site at http://www.studentparentjournal.com to share with others.

ENGAGE YOUR CHILD IN YOUR EDUCATIONAL EXPERIENCE

How many kids can say, "I went to college when I was two"? Children learn to emulate their parents. You are their first teachers. What you do, they want to do. What you say, they want to say. Their little minds are like sponges that soak up and retain information. Allow your children to enjoy the benefits of what you're learning, especially if they are wide awake and not ready for bed yet.

If you're studying a second language, let your child hold up the flashcards while you speak the words out loud. If you're reading a textbook, make sure he has children's books to read or picture books to browse through if he's not old enough to read yet. If you're doing math homework, cut up some fruit or vegetables and have her count and eat. Let these activities be fun. If she is fussy and not in the mood, don't force her. Think of other creative and fun ways to include your little "busy body" in your homework and school activities at least until he falls asleep. Before you know it, you may have a little scholar on your hands.

Children who experience college with you will learn the value of higher education at a very early age. No matter how busy you are, incorporate time into your busy schedule to read to your child every day. This activity can be your special snuggling and bonding time at the end of a hectic day. Reading to your child regularly will help your little one grow her vocabulary, create a desire to read, and become a confident learner.[2] She will become well prepared for kindergarten and be likely to attend college herself. Wouldn't that make you proud?

> **DID YOU KNOW?**
>
> Children begin learning at birth. As a general guide you can follow these early learning milestones as your child grows:
>
> - Recognizes your voice between zero and four months old
> - Responds to sounds between six months and twelve months
> - Understands words between eight months and eleven months
> - Says first words between twelve months and nineteen months
> - Vocabulary increases, uses short sentences from fifteen months to twenty-four months[1]
>
> Every child is different and may reach these milestones at other ages. This is used as a guide. For a more comprehensive list of other milestone activities and their time line, see appendix A— Early Learning for a list of Web sites.

MOMMY, PLAY WITH ME

As you journey through your college years, time with your child becomes scarce and valuable. Even though you may feel guilty about doing homework all the time, your child simply enjoys the love and security of being with you. Whether you're tickling him on the bed during breaks from typing your term paper or snuggling under a blanket watching her favorite Disney movie, children love attention and affection.

Spending time with your child doesn't have to include elaborate and expensive outings. Look for free and low-cost activities in your community. Walks in the park, drives across town, and rides on the bus can become learning explorations. For example, ask your child to tell you the colors and shapes of signs, cars, lights, and pictures you see when you're outdoors or at home. Make learning play and have fun, even if your time is limited.

What kinds of activities do you do with your child?

Keeping it REAL

_____

_____

_____

_____

_____

Do you involve your child in your school and social activities so that you can spend more time together? How?

_____

_____

_____

_____

_____

Professor, May I Bring My Baby to Class?

I NEED SOME "ME" TIME

After spending quality "mommy" time with your child, you'll need some "me" time to stay sane. Even though your schedule is extra busy, you need time for you. Try to fit in activities that help you relax. For example, take in a movie, walk in the park, attend a girls night out with friends, go dancing, or read a magazine or book you enjoy. (Or maybe not. You have enough books to read for school!)

The keys to reducing stress are planning and organizing. Exercising is also extremely helpful. But the best cure for stress is not a massage, although that would be wonderful. It's much simpler and doesn't cost you anything. It's a good hearty laugh. Yes, laughter will kill that stress in a minute. Having trouble thinking of something to laugh about? Close your eyes, take a deep breath, and remember the last antic your child did to make you laugh out loud (LOL)! Are you laughing yet? Go ahead, LOL again.

What did your child do to make you laugh or smile?

_____

_____

_____

Keeping it REAL

What do you like to do for fun and relaxation?

_____

_____

_____

_____

ENCOURAGE YOURSELF

Only you know how much you can handle. If you decide to take a break from school, my only hope is that your break doesn't last a lifetime. Yes, life is going to get rough, and you will feel like giving up. Don't be too quick to quit. My mom used to tell me, "It's not as long as it has been and not as short as it's going to get." Think about that for a minute. Last year at this time, you had two years left of school. Now you have only one year left. "You're almost there," she'd say. My mom was and still is my biggest cheerleader. I hear her voice all the time. Have someone in your corner to encourage you when you feel like giving up. If nobody is around, encourage yourself.

Think of yourself on a swing. If no one is there to push you, what do you do? You start by moving your legs back and forth, back and forth, until you build momentum. Now don't forget to tighten up those buttocks and get your upper body moving too. Soon you'll find yourself smiling and swinging with the wind. And you did it all by yourself. To go higher you must keep working your legs, keep pushing yourself. Soon the momentum of your body working with gravity will take you to new heights. Don't give up. Keep pushing, keep swinging. Remember to tap in to the Power of You.

Why is it important for you to continue your education?

_____

_____

_____

_____

Keeping it REAL

Professor, May I Bring My Baby to Class?

Are you ready to learn how others managed their lives? Read these real-life stories of mothers who made many sacrifices to become successful students while making adjustments to spend quality time with their children.

Meet**Annette**

I hated high school. I had no intention of attending college. I was going to tackle life my way, and I did. The two years after high school were a blur of parties and long days selling women's clothes at a department store. I struggled to pay rent, car payments, and insurance. One morning I woke up sick, and it was not from drinking the night before. That spring, one month before I turned twenty-one, I gave birth to a blond, energetic baby boy with deep brown eyes and a beautiful smile. Many of my friends, who also said they hated high school, were completing their second year of college.

Annette Sokolnicki is a mother whose son reminded her years later the impact her education had on his life.

After Aaron was born, I still thought I could make my own way, living with my new husband, struggling to pay the bills for three people. When Aaron was six months old, I decided to give up and go home. My mother did not react like I had expected. She explained that I had one month to find an apartment, get out, and grow up. That seemed impossible. I had no money, no skills, and on my left hip was a drooling little boy with chubby legs who was just learning to crawl. I wanted her to take care of me, of us, but she said no and forced me to learn how to take care of myself and my baby.

Over the course of the month, I managed to get a job at a retail store and began to navigate the financial aid systems for welfare and college.

I was a stressed-out, stretched-out single mom. I worked my job, went to class, and then stayed up late many nights writing and studying. Aaron spent long days at the babysitter. I dragged him on Saturdays to the campus computer lab, and he spent many afternoons drawing or playing with LEGOs at the desk behind me. Money was always an issue. Some mornings before I headed for school, I would sit on our living room floor and count pennies to buy gas to get to class sixty miles away. Purchasing textbooks was more important than buying Aaron extras like the latest action figure. Some months I barely had enough to keep the lights on and food on the table.

Many nights I went to sleep feeling like a bad mom who neglected my child. But did Aaron remember any of that? I wondered, so I asked. He remembers camping in the spring at the lake: setting up the tent, making fires, and snuggling into our sleeping bags and listening to the night sounds of the crickets and frogs. He remembers taking his little plastic table and chairs to the campground, and how, when one of those chairs got too close to the campfire, the heat made the plastic chair look like a melting marshmallow.

> *Many nights I went to sleep feeling like a bad mom who neglected my child. But, did Aaron remember any of that?*

He remembers spending summer afternoons hanging off the end of Grandma's dock, fishing. When the little fish would eat his worm off his big hook, I would cut the next piece of worm with my fingernail and maneuver that gross wiggly thing onto his hook. I hated it! He remembers that I hated it, but I did it anyway.

He also remembers fall afternoon walks in the woods with Grandma and me and stopping on the way home at a small pizza house. Before he even finished telling me his memories, I was crying. I had been carrying around all this guilt of being a bad, neglectful mother! Although we had many hard times, he had wonderful memories of his early childhood. I graduated with a bachelor's degree in communications at the same time Aaron graduated from kindergarten.

Next month I am flying to Connecticut to see Aaron to celebrate his twenty-first birthday. Aaron and I are good friends and enjoy spending time together. When he was a baby, his beautiful face and his contagious smile encouraged me. Today, Aaron still has that smile. Aaron says he loves telling his friends that I work in family medicine research and that someday I would like to complete a PhD. I love bragging about Aaron and his accomplishments. He is attending college and looking to do something in the medical field.

Annette Sokolnicki lives with her husband and children in East Lansing, Michigan. She is a master gardener, loves growing flowers, cooking, and playing with her children. Annette is currently the project manager for a National Institutes of Health study in medical anthropology. She is completing her master's degree and plans to apply to Michigan State University's Community and Ecological doctorate program.

Meet**Rasheedah**

About five years ago, shortly before graduating from high school, I set two major goals for myself that I was determined to accomplish. The first was to be the first person in my family to graduate from college by completing my undergraduate education at Temple University; the second goal was to gain admission to Temple University's prestigious Beasley School of Law and become an attorney. I knew my ambitions would require the qualities of hard work, perseverance, relentlessness, and dedication, all of which I was prepared to give forth with every breath in my body. These goals, however, were infinitely complicated by the fact that I had a four-year-old child to take care of.

My daughter, Iyonna, was born when I was fourteen years old and in the ninth grade. Coming from a family of teen mothers, I was determined to be the first in my family to break the cycle and to achieve a college degree. Although I was ultimately successful in high school with support from my mother and teachers, being a full-time parent to Iyonna while being a full-time college student presented many more struggles than I had anticipated. There were the matters

Rasheedah Phillips is a mother who recognized at an early age that her education would change her daughter's destiny.

of how I was going to afford to go to college, where my child and I would live, who was going to care for her during classes, how I was going to be able to afford her child care and other living expenses, how I was going to be able to maintain a hectic schedule in order to graduate early, and many other concerns. These issues threatened to discourage me from continuing my education, threatened to defer my dreams. But I've been told two truisms in life that, although seemingly cliché, have become powerful truths in my life: where there is a will, there is a way, and if you want something bad enough, you must make the necessary sacrifices in order to achieve it.

All of my goals, dreams, and intentions were realized—I began my journey of higher education at Temple University during the fall semester of 2002. In order to achieve my goal of graduating early, I managed a courseload of eighteen credits per semester, as well as attending summer classes. I was able to receive a number of scholarships and a few school loans to help with living expenses and had to work part-time jobs in order to take care of other expenses. Not wanting to limit my college experience, I decided

I was able to earn a 3.79 GPA, graduating summa cum laude from Temple in three years, and, in the fall of 2005, I matriculated at Temple University Beasley School of Law.

to join school organizations, begin my own student organization, and participate in community service, making time to speak to organizations like Communities In Schools about my experiences as a young mother in college. I mentor young parents and tell them that success is still possible in spite of their personal challenges. I have also worked with community organizations on projects geared toward making adolescents more sexually aware, informing them of the importance of living adolescence to the fullest, and obtaining an education before they consider having a child.

I was able to earn a 3.79 GPA, graduating summa cum laude from Temple in three years, and, in the fall of 2005, I matriculated at Temple University Beasley School of Law.

In order to juggle my many responsibilities, it was necessary for me to have quality, reliable day care for my child in a facility that I could trust to provide her with a safe environment, educational and cultural enrichment, and nurturance. However, relying upon school loans and scholarships to meet our living expenses, the cost of day care far exceeded my budget. During my senior year in high school, a counselor encouraged me to apply for the Family Care Solutions child care scholarship, which provided financial assistance for day care expenses for mothers enrolled in college. I was granted the scholarship in 2002 during my freshman year and was fortunate to get continued support while going to law school. The child care scholarship gave me one less financial burden to worry about, allowing me to focus on my studies rather than on struggling to find affordable day care while I worked and went to school.

There are many young parents who have been discouraged by their circumstances, who have been told and who believe that they cannot realize their goals and dreams. Many of us were forced to mature at very young ages, to face responsibilities and situations that we shouldn't have had to face. Many of us had to give up our childhood before we even had a chance to taste it. Many of us made wrong choices and made mistakes because of the limited choices that we had to begin with and not being able to perceive the opportunities laid out before us. Many of us are part of a vicious, oppressive cycle— that of poverty, drugs, teen parenthood, abuse, no parents, gangs, jail, unemployment. We come from broken environments, desolate neighborhoods filled with hopelessness, frustration, desperation— the products and victims of inequality, racism, classism, sexism, elitism. We have been told that we wouldn't amount to much, that we would not get very far, that we have no worth or value, and we have internalized these views, adopted them as our own. Do not let your life's circumstances define or confine you. Instead, use them as motivation to overachieve and rise above those expectations. You can still be that artist, that engineer, that doctor, that lawyer that you dreamed of being as a child. Your presence, your perseverance will serve to counter the erroneous thinking of many people who hold preconceived notions that our past mistakes prevent any hope for success as adults. You must fight to dispel the countless stereotypes and statistics that burden you and to defy every figure and number calculated. Let it not be merely the satisfaction of achievement that drives you but the discontent of accepting a fate that others have created for you.

Rasheedah Phillips graduated from Temple University Beasley School of Law in May 2008. She has a daughter, Iyonna. She is working as a public interest attorney and plans to continue working with young teens to inform them of their legal rights in regard to their children. When she's not plotting to save the world, Rasheedah enjoys writing stories, traveling, and taking long walks through the park.

Meet**Kassandra**

On the morning of September 11, 2001, I roused my nearly nine-month-old daughter, Samantha, and put her in her highchair. She, as usual, clapped and giggled and spoke to me in her own language as I prepared her breakfast. When Cheerios appeared on her tray table, she began to bounce in excitement and gurgled at me in appreciation. My heart swelled at the knowledge that we had finally, in that early September, left Samantha's abusive father and moved to a tiny student apartment of our own. I would be starting as a freshman at prestigious Lawrence University the following week. Any doubts I had had about my ability to provide for Samantha while juggling work and a heavy student load subsided as I stood in my own apartment, watching my beautiful daughter celebrate the wonder of Cheerios. I had planned to take Samantha to the library that day, as nothing pleased my girl more than taking books off a shelf, chewing on them a bit, looking at the pictures, and watching me put them back. Then I turned on the television.

Kassandra Kuehl is a mother who engaged her child in her academic world.

Professor, May I Bring My Baby to Class?

It would have been easy to sit in front of the television for the entire day, the entire week, the rest of my life. I, like the rest of the nation, suddenly lost all sense of security, of focus, of direction. I didn't want to think, to question, to move. I just wanted the television to tell me what was happening to my world until I could make some sense out of it. But I had an obligation to turn off the television that day because on September 11, 2001, Samantha learned to crawl.

There were many moments, hours, and even days during my college career when it would have been easy to simply curl up and insist that everything stop until I had time to process it all. Instead, Samantha and I learned to adjust. She learned to walk, to speak, to have an opinion. We went on field trips to the zoo with her preschool on the way to campaign rallies. We went from her dance classes and swimming lessons to the house where I tutored at-risk high-school-aged men. And we went from my dance rehearsals to Amnesty International meetings, sorority functions, and work, before going back home, where we learned that snuggling is an activity not to be missed.

> *Samantha was never still again, and rather than wish that she be still so I could focus, I learned to focus on the run.*

Samantha was never still again, and rather than wish that she be still so I could focus, I learned to focus on the run. I learned to study foreign vocabulary by letting her hold up the flashcards, learned that being an activist and a mother at the same time is a lot easier if you give your child a set of pompoms to wave at rallies, and learned that a forty-hour workweek on top of a full class load and several extracurricular activities is possible if you pick work and activities that can amuse a toddler.

I am currently finishing my final year of law school, and Samantha is almost seven years old. The world continues to spin, and Samantha and I have learned to love spinning with it. I don't sleep much, my budget is tight, and I study so hard that I have constant headaches.

Yet somehow, I know that it will be worth it when I walk across the stage at graduation, and my daughter is as transfixed by me as I was with her on the day she began to crawl.

Kassandra Kuehl is a writer and playwright who currently resides with her daughter, Samantha, in Mountain View, California. Kassandra graduated magna cum laude from Lawrence University in 2005 and in 2008 earned a degree in international law from the University of California Hastings College of the Law. Kassandra is a human rights activist, dancer, and volunteer infant "cuddler" at UCSF Children's Hospital.

Meet**Michelle**

"I have been accepted into Michigan State University, and I hope to go in January [2000]. The costs are adding up. I can't believe how much money it takes and how little I have. I'm not sure how I will manage it all, but I really feel as though I have no choice. What kind of life can I ask for my child if I don't have a good education? I want to give her the best I can. I am terrified I won't have the strength to do it. But, just think, four years from now, I might just have a bachelor's degree. Wow."

—Diary entry, 9/2/99

Michelle Artibee is a mother who learned to make adjustments where necessary to stay focused.

The above entry was written three weeks before the birth of my daughter, Katelyn. I was eighteen years old and had graduated high school a few months prior. There is a common theme in my diary entries during that time: a lot of fear.

I could give you the history of Katelyn's father (absent from our lives), my experiences as a pregnant teenager, how my family reacted, and so on, but I would prefer to focus on my life as a student-parent, in hopes that it will reach someone who's either considering college or going through it now, while pregnant or already parenting.

On New Year's Day of 2000 I moved into a family housing apartment at Michigan State University in East Lansing, Michigan,

Professor, May I Bring My Baby to Class?

four hours away from my family and small hometown, with a three-month-old baby in tow. I had a large, messy ball of doubt and terror nesting in the pit of my stomach. I cried when my parents left the following day after helping me unpack.

Despite all of my anxiety and doubt, I carved out a new life for us. I found child care and employment, registered for classes, eventually learned my way around the area, and met others, through Michigan State University's student-parent organization, that were living a life similar to mine. At times it was very overwhelming, especially when my daughter became ill with typical childhood illnesses.

After a year and a half of taking courses at Michigan State University and dealing with chronic ear infections that my daughter had, I realized that Michigan State University may not have been the best choice for me. The auditorium-style courses with six hundred fellow students intimidated me, I felt isolated in my classes because of my lifestyle, and I missed a lot of classes and work because of Katelyn being sick.

An opportunity arose to work full time in the campus department where I was a student-employee, the Family Resource Center. Ironically this is the office that helps support students with children, yet even while working in the office, I knew I had to change my educational plan.

Since I was working full time, I needed an alternative to traditional classes. I found an on-line program through Lansing Community College that I enrolled in. After a year and a half, I obtained a general associate degree and graduated with honors. What I remember most about that graduation ceremony was sitting there and realizing that I had finally made progress on the goal I set out to achieve. I felt empowered.

Two years later I earned a bachelor of science degree in digital communication at Franklin University, located in Columbus, Ohio. The courses for this degree were also offered 100 percent on-line, so my first day on campus was actually my graduation day!

I continued to work for the Family Resource Center at Michigan State University full time while going to school. With my degrees, I've moved up the pay scale significantly over the past five years. In May 2007, I earned my master's degree in business administration from Baker College in Flint, Michigan. After completing my educational plan (hallelujah!), I started job hunting. While this transition was more difficult than I anticipated, I knew the right "fit" would come in due time.

I will not sugarcoat the lifestyle of a student-parent. It is chaotic, it is at times very unnerving, and yes, it can be extremely hard. I remember one night while rubbing my daughter's back for over an hour (she didn't feel good and was having such a hard time falling asleep) when I collapsed in tears. I had assignments due by midnight, and it was already 11:00 p.m. I was operating on fumes and exhausted. There weren't enough hours in the day to accomplish everything I needed to, and I simply lost it.

I want her to learn the importance of never surrendering to the expectations other people have of you.

But then Katelyn crawled into my lap to give me a hug. In that moment, I stopped thinking about deadlines and exhaustion and remembered why I was doing all of it to begin with. My beautiful daughter, who had asked for nothing but love and care from me when she was born, was my reason. Our life and future together as a family was the most important thing to me. I refused to be another statistic of an unwed mother raising a family on welfare. I refused to give her less than my best. Though being able to provide her with "extras" in life is a nice thought, I am motivated by something larger than that.

I want her to learn the importance of never surrendering to the expectations other people have of you. What is important is that you achieve the expectations you set for yourself. I want her to always know that she and I are a family and that we are complete the way we are. We're a team, and we don't give up on each other, no matter how challenging the obstacles may be. Katelyn may remember very little (if any) of our life as a student-parent family, and that is okay. I will

Professor, May I Bring My Baby to Class?

remember for the both of us and know in my heart that I've given her everything I possibly could.

Michelle Artibee presently lives in central New York and is employed at Cornell University as the associate director for work/life programs. She earned an associate degree in 2003 from Lansing Community College, a bachelor's degree in 2004 from Franklin University, and a master of business administration in 2007 from Baker College. Michelle enjoys spending time in her craft room, visiting the beautiful waterfalls of central New York, reading, and above all, being with her family and friends.

Meet**LaKeesha**

When I was seventeen years old and a high school senior, I found out that I was pregnant. I was one of the captains of the varsity basketball team and was looking at full scholarships to many division II and III colleges along the east coast.

LaKeesha Holloman is a mother who played college basketball, worked, and went to school.

I managed to graduate high school in June, and not too long after that, I turned down my first- and second-choice division II colleges. In August, I was a new single mother.

Even though I had the most supportive family in the world, this was still the scariest time in my life. I decided to go to a local community college soon after my daughter was born, and there I started out studying computer technology and playing for the college basketball team. I went through the first few semesters with a child to come home to at night and classes to go to in the morning. I also worked a part-time job at the local Rite Aid. I lived with my parents at this time, and my mother cared for my daughter while I worked or was in school.

The schedule went a little like this: morning class, home for lunch and afternoon baby feeding (if I was lucky enough to make it home before she went down for her nap), evening class, evening basketball practice (or an out-of-town game), and home for baby's bath, my shower, and some late-evening studying (with an occasional midnight feeding). On the weekends I'd try to get as many hours in at the pharmacy as possible.

I struggled with school and life for a while; I even stopped attending college for a semester here and there. I must have changed my major a million times. I just didn't know what or who I wanted to be at that time. I also struggled with occasional moments of regrets. I wouldn't call it regret so much, but I guess more like the thought of "where would I be if …"

I took my daughter to class with me one time in her early baby stages and quite a few times when she was old enough to occupy herself. I missed plenty of classes for reasons such as diaper rash, fever, cold, runny nose, and baby checkups, and add a few more for sleep deprivation. Even when my daughter wasn't with me, she was with me in my thoughts. I was always thinking of her and missing her, wondering what she was doing. Several times I laughed out loud during class just thinking about a silly thing she'd done the previous night.

Having children can change a lot of things and force one to make a lot of sacrifices. Having a child can also be a positive, life-altering event that helps you to become more focused on success. Knowing that my efforts are leading to success for myself and success for my children is the best feeling in the world. But even better is knowing how proud of me they will be some day.

In 2006, at age twenty-three, I managed to graduate from the same local community college that I had started at in 2000. It took a little longer than I intended, but I walked out of that arena not only with a degree but also the mother to a six-year-old little girl and a one-year-old boy.

Lakeesha Holloman lives in Lewiston, Maine, with her three children. She graduated from Central Maine Community College in May 2006 with a certificate as a medical assistant. She plans to go back to school to become a nurse. Lakeesha enjoys being with her family and playing basketball.

Professor, May I Bring My Baby to Class?

Meet**Rita**

I have two sons. My youngest, KC, was born in July 2004. Shortly after his birth, I was told he might have a heart murmur, and he needed extra care until the doctors could conclusively determine the problem. I was attending Community College of Philadelphia at the time but was not deterred. With the support of my family, I continued my education at Drexel University. It was tough for me to make the decision to go back to school. I was afraid to leave KC because of his medical condition.

In my joyous moments, my children are laughing with me, and when I am downcast, they are asking, "What's wrong, Mommy?" They encourage me to hang in there. My children started cooperating with me at a very tender age and understand that Mom is busy with schoolwork. Going to college with KC in day care has been a joy. He actively participates in the markings and drawings on my notebook. When he's done, he falls asleep in my arms with books scattered all over the place. I stare at him apologetically with tears rolling down from my eyes, thinking that I have not given him enough attention. Little did I know KC would develop a love for books through this process. He started ahead of his classmates at the day care center. He watches less television and would rather fondle his books or draw lines on a notebook. He is already saying he wants to be a medical doctor.

I realize that my going to school will pave the way for our greatness in the future. This is the only way I am able to compete and give my kids a better tomorrow. I cherish my experience of parenting while going to college and wouldn't trade it for anything.

Rita Anusionwu is the proud mother of two boys. She was born in Umuode, Nsulu Abia State, Nigeria, Africa. Rita migrated to America in 1999 after having won a visa lottery. She and her husband are raising their children in Philadelphia, Pennsylvania. Rita graduated from Drexel University in June of 2009 earning her bachelor's degree in nursing. She enjoys reading, cooking, dancing, and entertaining friends.

Rita Anusionwu is a mother whose toddler developed a love for books and says he wants to be a doctor.

Meet Roslinda

I am a twenty-six-year-old full-time single mother and eligibility worker and a part-time student. On February 18, 2004, I gave birth to a beautiful baby boy, and I named him Chance. Chance was born with hypoplastic left heart syndrome. In case you are not familiar with this term, the condition is a congenital heart disease where the left side of the heart does not develop. I found out about his condition close to my due date. It was explained to me that Chance would need three surgeries that would be performed in stages. Chance was scheduled to have his first open-heart surgery two days after birth, the second at six months of age, and the third one between twelve and eighteen months of age. At that point I thought I had some relief because I was given a schedule. But then Chance underwent two surgeries within the first five days of life, which is when I realized that a schedule was nothing to count on. I stayed at the hospital night and day until he was able to go home after the second surgery was complete.

While Chance was hospitalized, I lost two jobs, an apartment, time with his dad and my friends, and most of all, time for school. I moved in with an aunt, and boy, she did not make it easy. She was one of those people who complained about everything. I remember sitting in her living room, and she asked me when I was going back to work. I said to her, "I am going back to school." Quiet filled the room. Then she said that school would be a good idea, and she started telling me about how she obtained her GED the same year that her oldest daughter was graduating from high school.

I soon weighed my options and took advantage of all the programs that Pennsylvania had to offer. I had limited funds so I applied for welfare, which gave me medical insurance, food stamps, and cash benefits

Roslinda Harris is a mother who continues her education despite her baby's health challenges.

> *But then Chance underwent two surgeries within the first five days of life, which is when I realized that a schedule was nothing to count on.*

Professor, May I Bring My Baby to Class?

for my son and me. The Department of Public Welfare helped a lot. It helped me obtain social security benefits and find day care centers that were able to care for my son and his condition and accepted subsidized child care. Because my curriculum was nursing, the Department of Public Welfare paid for me to go and recertify my CNA (certified nursing assistant) license, which had also expired during my pregnancy. That CNA license allowed me to get a full-time nurse's aide position at a nursing home, which allowed me to start back to school part time.

Three years have passed, and Chance has not received his last surgery. I always kept a good-paying job and stayed in school, but one thing that still remains is that his surgery is going to happen when I least expect it to. I have utilized my in-between time to get a head start on my education because if I had sat around waiting on that last surgery, I just would have been pushed back another two years in my educational goals. I'm graduating in a few months with my associate degree. This degree will help me get a better paying, more flexible job that will allow me to go back to school full time during the day to finish out my nursing degree. The reason for saying that I am a full-time mom is because I really am. You can be too, while setting goals and utilizing your time wisely. I get up every morning before 5:00 a.m. to get my son ready. Remember to always pray and put God first, and He will never steer you wrong. Seeing my son smile every morning and every night before bed lets me know that everything that I do is just for him. There will always be hills in your life. Just start with the small ones and everything will work out just fine.

Roslinda Harris lives in Philadelphia, Pennsylvania, with her son, Chance. She is a 2009 graduate of the Metropolitan Career Center. Roslinda earned an associate degree in specialized technology with a focus on hardware, software, and Web design. She enjoys reading, cooking, and spending time with her son.

CHAPTER 5

I'm Pregnant This Semester— Now What?

Whether you're a freshman, sophomore, junior, or senior in college, being pregnant may make you feel scared and uncertain, but it does not have to mean defeat. Having your baby while going to college may slow your progress down a bit, but remember you are still the same person—strong willed, intelligent, and a college student.

Your life is certainly going to be different. Your emotions will take you on a roller-coaster ride. At any time you may feel nervous, sad, excited, confused, worried, joyful, or depressed. The stresses of maintaining your regular class schedule and activities, studying, being in a relationship, and coping with mounting family conflicts add to the pressure.

You have so much to consider. Do you have to move out of your dorm? Where will you go? Before you become overwhelmed with questions, first, take care of yourself. Schedule an appointment to see a prenatal-care physician or healthcare provider as soon as possible and keep all your follow-up appointments. Seeing a doctor or prenatal provider regularly is key to keeping you and your baby healthy. Early intervention can detect health problems that, without treatment, may become serious later. When your baby is born, it's also important that she or he sees a healthcare provider. Regular checkups with a

I really don't think life is about the I-could-have-beens. Life is only about the I-tried-to-do. I don't mind the failure but I can't imagine that I'd forgive myself if I didn't try.

Nikki Giovanni

healthcare provider and pediatric dentist can prevent, detect, and treat health problems.

Next, surround yourself with positive people who will provide encouragement and support. Begin planning now. Consider what adjustments you need to make to your daily activities and class schedule for next semester. You may decide to take off a semester or two, or depending on when your baby is due and your health, you may be able to jump right back into school without missing a beat.

SHARING THE NEWS

The unexpected has happened, just when you were getting into the groove of your life as a college student. Everyone was so exited about you being a college student. You are maintaining good grades. You finally started participating in school activities. You've maintained a good balance between academics and your social life. You are enjoying the college experience. And now, well, a baby is on the way. What are you going to do? Assuming your pregnancy was unplanned, I'm also assuming that maybe at some point you felt regretful, disappointed, and shameful. After internalizing, processing, and examining the situation you think, what does all this mean? How may it alter your future? Your most pressing challenge at the moment is sharing the news with your boyfriend and with your parents. What do you say? How do you say it? When do you tell them?

> **DID YOU KNOW?**
>
> About one quarter of undergraduates in college during the 2003–04 academic year had one or more dependents, and 13 percent were single parents.[1]

The disappointments you're sure they all will experience weigh heavily on your heart, and those emotions make it difficult to concentrate, be jubilant, and well, just be yourself. You may be tempted to hide your pregnancy from your family, peers, and professors. You know how especially proud they are of you for becoming the first in the family to go to college or maybe for earning a full scholarship or maybe because you've adjusted so well while

Professor, May I Bring My Baby to Class?

attending school out of state. You constantly think of how you should break the news. Should you tell them in person, over the phone, through e-mail, or have a friend or another family member tell them? Telling your boyfriend that you're pregnant may not seem as difficult as sharing the news with your mother and father.

Your relationship with your parents and your comfort level with them will determine how you share the news. My husband and I found out about my stepdaughter's pregnancy over the phone. It worked best for her comfort level and for my husband, who didn't have to respond right away. He had time to process the news and talk with his daughter at a later time. I'm not suggesting that this is the right way or wrong way. You will have to decide the best way and the most respectful way to share the news about your pregnancy.

I believe it's best to share the news early on. It will help relieve some of the anxiety and sadness you may be feeling. I'm sure most people want to see you succeed and will support you any way they can. Remember to listen to the Power of You.

If I am way off base about your feelings and reaction to your pregnancy, and you were ecstatic about your pregnancy, then please accept my apologies and continue to read.

BUILD A SUPPORT SYSTEM

I participated in a wonderful exercise designed to see how well a group of leaders worked together. Ten people participated, all of whom I am friends with, each with different personalities and different styles of leadership. The exercise was to put together a three-hundred piece puzzle in thirty minutes. We all immediately went to work, enthusiastic and ready to tackle the task at hand. One member, who never seems to have a care in the world, took charge and said, "Let's do the border first." Another said, "I love doing puzzles." Another said, "Give me all the reds." I asked for the blues and pinks. It was amazing. We became one, like the members of your body (your arms, hands, legs, and feet) performing many functions and supporting each other to achieve a single goal. The puzzle was completed faster by all of us working together than it ever could have been completed by any one of us working alone. This exercise also taught me that you never know how people can contribute until you give them an opportunity to help.

The point I'm trying to make is that you need support and you shouldn't assume people can't or won't help you, until you've asked. Try this—make a list of all those whom you trust and are close to: the baby's father, family members, friends, and classmates. Sit down with them individually and let them know that you hope they will support you on your journey through college. It's always a good idea to surround yourself with positive people who will motivate you and cheer you on.

As we worked through the puzzle exercise, one team member was always encouraging us. "You are doing a great job. Don't worry about the time—that's not important. Just keep working." He was right. Time often isn't as important as completing the task itself. We can get so caught up in finishing something in a certain time frame that we put unnecessary pressure on ourselves and sometimes give up before we start. It's good to use time as a reference to establish when we want to achieve our goal, but if it doesn't happen when we want it to, does that mean we give up? Never! Keep in mind that stuff happens and your schedule may be delayed.

When your life gets a little hectic while pursuing your goal, just remind yourself of what you're working toward. Picture what you're trying to make out of life's puzzle pieces. Visualize that degree over and over again. Look at your son or daughter and remember why you are working so hard. "Great job," I heard. "Keep working. Don't worry about the time—it's not important." I learned that we all need people in our lives to help us succeed. It was great to come together, supporting one another to accomplish one task. Oh, by the way, we didn't finish in thirty minutes but we were determined to finish, and we did.

Once you have identified a support team, call a meeting to discuss your plans. To make it fun, call it a "support me in college party" and serve refreshments. Make sure everyone is introduced and is comfortable with one another. Create your schedule using the Managing My Schedule template in appendix C. It may be better for team members to make commitments over a semester as opposed to the academic year. Your team can rotate assignments each semester or trimester. List your support team members on the calendar on page 170 in appendix C. Copy and share it with others. You may also print a blank table from our Web site, http://www.studentparentjournal.com. A support team means that you don't have to rely on just one person to handle unexpected circumstances or emergencies and that one support person isn't pressured into handling all your needs. For example, if the child care provider calls to say that the center is closed because the facility's heater is broken on the day of your final exam, you will need more than one backup option. Everyone on your support team should get a copy of the Managing My Schedule calendar along with phone numbers. Having a support system should make life a little easier for you.

TIME MANAGEMENT

Consider informing your professors about your pregnancy early on so that they may be more sympathetic if you miss class because you have morning sickness. Identify a classmate or two who don't mind sharing and reviewing notes with you when you are absent. Know your limits. Try not to take on more than you can handle. Stress can affect your health. Talk to your advisor about your class load, work schedule, and other activities. You may need to drop a class, cut back on work hours, reduce your extracurricular activities, or take a break from school. Or if you're like some of the women featured in this book, you may be able to maintain balance, focus, a healthy pregnancy, and your daily schedule without changing much at all.

TAKING TIME OFF

If you are planning to take time off from school for a semester or longer and want to stay connected to school, consider taking on-line courses. This will help you continue to earn credits while you are at home enjoying your newborn. However, if you truly want to take a break from school, well, that's more time to enjoy your new baby. Whatever you decide to do, do it because you believe it is the right plan for you, not because you are being pressured to stay in school or take a break from school. Remember to listen to the Power of You.

PREPARE NOW FOR YOUR RETURN TO COLLEGE

If you are considering taking a break from school, begin preparing now, while you are still on campus, for your return. Begin calling around on campus to identify student-parent support services like child care, student-parent housing, and financial assistance. Be persistent. Some colleges and universities are huge, so it might take some research to find which office you should call to find out what, if any, student-parent support services your college offers. If your school has an on-campus child care center, that's probably the best place to start. Next, try the women's center, followed by the offices of financial aid, student affairs, or institutional advancement. Search your school's Web site as well. Refer to the previous chapters for information to help in your search for child care and other support services for student-parents. Connect with other student-parents on campus to see what resources they use. Check with your advisor to learn how your sabbatical may affect your financial aid, grants, scholarships, or work study. Take care of as much of this type of planning as you can now so that coming back to school is an easier transition.

The day I learned I was pregnant, I thought

_____

_____

_____

_____

_____

_____

Keeping it REAL

The day I told my partner I was pregnant, he said

_____

_____

_____

_____

Now that I'm pregnant, I plan to

_____

_____

_____

_____

_____

_____

I LEARNED I WAS PREGNANT (continued)

How could moving back home help or hinder me?

Keeping it REAL

_____

_____

_____

_____

_____

_____

I plan to get an apartment because

_____

_____

_____

_____

_____

_____

I can depend on my baby's father to

_____

_____

_____

_____

_____

_____

I can depend on my baby's father's family to

_____

_____

_____

_____

_____

Keeping it REAL

I've spoken to the following people who have offered to provide support during my pregnancy and/or help care for my baby following birth:

_____

_____

_____

_____

_____

I've decided to continue school next semester as a full-time or part-time student (choose one) because

_____

_____

_____

_____

_____

I've decided to keep going or take time off from school because (choose one)

_____

_____

_____

_____

_____

_____

_____

Keeping it REAL

My school provides the following support services for student-parents:

_____

_____

_____

_____

_____

_____

_____

_____

_____

_____

Are you ready to exercise the Power of You? Read these real-life stories about courageous mothers who didn't give up their dreams of earning a college degree when they learned they were pregnant. Be encouraged and know that anything is possible.

Meet Ayesha

When I think back to the day that I first found out I was pregnant, the first thought that comes to mind is fear. Even though my parents were divorced, I was always the one who maintained a close relationship with both sides. I wasn't fearful for the punishment I would face but fearful for the disappointment I would cause. Both of my parents are graduates of Lincoln University, which was my college of choice for a few reasons, most of all for the fact that I would receive the alumni discount of 50 percent off of the current tuition.

Ayesha Mosee is a mother who didn't give up her dreams of earning a college degree after her baby was born.

I was very eager to stay on campus; I thought of it like my own apartment with a roommate who was actually one of my best friends from high school. What more could I ask for? We shopped for matching comforter sets, decorations for our dorm room, even our own cleaning supplies, we were so excited! Well, the first or second weekend after the semester began, I came home for a doctor's appointment and learned that I was pregnant. What was I going to do? I was very confused and disappointed at the same time. However, for some reason I was constantly thinking about the future of my unborn child. What kind of future would I be able to provide with limited education? How would I support my child without a job? Where would we live? How would we survive? These were all of the questions racing through my head.

Once I finally got the courage to tell my family, I had a mixture of responses. While everyone may have been disappointed, no one ever turned their back on me. My parents and stepmother weren't too thrilled about becoming grandparents at such young ages but there was never a moment where that was displayed, with the exception of the initial conversation I had with them. I don't really remember my father's exact words over the phone when I gave him the news. However, I do remember the look on his face when I finally saw him after he knew that I was pregnant. It was that look of disappointment that I dreaded. The forty-five minutes that he and I were in the car together riding home from Lincoln felt like forever!

My mother, on the other hand, had a different way of dealing with it. She never gave me the impression that she was disappointed but rather that she was there for me. She was willing to do whatever it took to ensure that my unborn child would be taken care of. I knew that I would receive support from my father as well. I just think that it took him a little longer to get over the initial shock of becoming a grandfather at such a young age.

> *She was willing to do whatever it took to ensure that my unborn child would be taken care of.*

I managed to finish my first semester at Lincoln, and when I left in December, I had every intention of coming back in the fall. I had my son on February 18, 1996. He was eight pounds thirteen ounces—a very big boy. His father and I had our differences, but we finally decided on naming him Tahmir. He was the first boy in either of our families in a long time so naturally he was shown so much love.

As time went on, the day for me to go back to school approached. I was very skeptical about leaving my baby. I made the mistake of taking a semester off, which eventually turned into a year. I went back to Lincoln after one year and made the decision to stay on campus because I thought that would allow me to stay focused. My son's father and my mother worked out a schedule for Tahmir so she would keep him for part of the week and his dad would have him the other days. I made it my business to come home every weekend to spend time with Tahmir.

This routine went on for two semesters, and over the summer I finally got my first "real job." I was able to provide for my son and myself and that felt good. I was always able to count on my family for

Professor, May I Bring My Baby to Class?

support, but I felt like it was time for me to be able to provide support for my son. Once summer ended, I made the decision to continue working and not go back to Lincoln. I was on academic probation because I just couldn't stay focused. I enrolled at my local community college and took a few courses so that once I was ready to go back to Lincoln, I wouldn't be too far behind. While attending Community College of Philadelphia, I worked and was eventually offered a better-paying position. Once again I put my education on hold in order to provide a more financially stable environment for my son.

In 2001 I gave birth to my second child, a baby girl, Taliyah. Not only did I need to provide for my son but now my daughter as well. With a better-paying job, I, as most people do, became comfortable with my finances and lost sight of the importance of obtaining my degree. Putting my education on hold for a short period of time evolved into years, until in 2006 I decided it was time for me to go back to school and earn my degree! I enrolled in Peirce College under a cluster that was sponsored by my employer at the time. The college was very good with catering to the adult learner and offered very flexible schedules. It was a little difficult, at first, managing home, work, and school, but I managed. In June of 2008 I received my associate degree in business administration with a concentration in management, and I am currently at Peirce working toward my bachelor's. The educational journey has been very long for me, but I'm fine with that. At times I would get discouraged about not having my degree, but as long as I know that I am working toward my goal I am all right.

Today, I am very grateful for having such a supportive family, and I am also grateful for them allowing me to make mistakes. People often think that having a child at an early age is the end of the world. Trust me—it isn't. At this point in my life, everything I do is for my children. I wouldn't trade either of them for the world. I thank my parents for instilling family values, and for that reason, today I am leading by example!

Ayesha Mosee lives in Philadelphia, Pennsylvania, with her family. She has two children, Tahmir and Taliyah and a stepdaughter, Tyhira. She received an associate degree from Peirce College in 2008. Ayesha is working toward her bachelor's degree in business administration with a concentration in management. She expects to graduate in 2010. In her spare time she enjoys event planning, shopping, and spending time with family.

Meet**Rebecca**

What to Expect When You're Expecting was not written for women in college, young moms, or career women. Panicking and looking for answers, I began reading it after I found out I was pregnant. This book, while it raised valid points and gave some tips, did not tell me how I was to do it all, how my professors would react, where I could find affordable day care, or how to build a support system out of my plethora of often-drunken college buddies. I had to look elsewhere, and other books, like *The Modern Girl's Guide to Motherhood*, were not all that helpful either.

I found out I was pregnant as I began my second semester of my sophomore year. I was just nineteen and hardly ready for a baby. I was having fun, doing well in my classes, and planning my future. When that stick turned pink, my world turned upside down. Gone were keg parties, all-night study sessions, and my simple life. When I told my friends, each assumed I would have an abortion; after all, we are liberal, young pro-choice women of the twenty-first century. I knew all along I would have that baby and make it work.

I kept up my busy schedule, thinking I had to learn to do it all now and be prepared to just take my baby along for the ride. I mean, it couldn't be that hard, right? I was sure other women did this; I just couldn't find any of them. I started looking on my college's Web site, thinking surely other people had children and went to class and made it look easy even if it wasn't. I found Student Parents on a Mission,

Rebecca Precht is a student who became a mother in her junior year and learned to adjust and manage her schedule to stay on course for graduation.

Professor, May I Bring My Baby to Class?

an advocacy group of sorts, which provided resources and support for student-parents. I was relieved.

I began looking for apartments, day care, cribs, and all the other gear every baby seems to need. (Really, you need it, want it, or think you need it. The baby doesn't care.) I approached my due date and fall term with mixed emotions. Would I really be able to pull this off? Could I afford to be a student and raise a child? How would I know what to do? What if I'm a terrible mother?

After a short and intense labor, I had my baby boy. When the nurse put him on my chest, he looked at me and didn't cry, and I somehow knew it was going to be fine—that we would be fine.

I moved into my apartment and found a crib and a day care center. Through Student Parents on a Mission I discovered that if I remained in school full time, then the university would pay for day care. I relaxed and let myself enjoy my semester off with my baby, who never slept like the books suggested a newborn should, and cleaned my house as if I had suddenly developed some sort of obsessive-compulsive disorder.

I no longer felt like I always had to please other people. I learned that I need time to myself, time for my son, time for work, and time for my school.

Panic set in again when I went back to work and back to school that winter. Would I really be able to study, go to class, and raise my son? Would I be able to give him everything he needed and have enough time with him without letting my schoolwork suffer? Would my professors understand if he got sick and couldn't go to day care? Would I still be able to obsessively scrub the house lest this baby, who wasn't even on the floor, somehow got a hold of something and put it in his mouth?

It took some getting used to and some extreme time-management skill, but I managed to make it work, and I became a better student, a better mother, and a woman who could say no. I no longer felt like I always had to please other people. I learned that I need time to myself, time for my son, time for work, and time for my school. And to be honest, there are never enough hours in the day for all of it. So I learned to say no, and I learned to juggle.

I was lucky in all of this. I have a wonderful support system, the best day care, and the most understanding professors. I have learned I am human. I cannot do it all, but I try my hardest because I want my son to have a better life—a life I can give him if I have a degree. My son loves sitting on my lap trying to type with me while I'm writing a paper; it's cute and annoying at the same time. Panic still sets in every so often, but it isn't as extreme as the first semester I went back to school as a mother.

My son is now eighteen months old, and I have to say I love this age best of all. He's learning with me, and he's incredibly bright. I'm doing well in school, working, and spending as much time as I can just with my son. I can't wait to be done with school next year, but this has been the best learning experience that I could have ever had. I have patience and management and budgeting skills I never had a couple of years ago. I now know I can do anything and be a better woman and mother for it. My son will be a better person for it. Soon I'll have a degree to go along with my new skills, and I will make an excellent ombudsman-soccer mom.

Rebecca Precht is a graduate of James Madison College at Michigan State University. She earned her bachelor's degree in May 2008 as a dual major in anthropology and social relations and policy. Rebecca is currently attending graduate school for social work at Wayne State University. She lives in Plymouth, Michigan, with her son.

Meet Tiffany

My son was a gift conceived from an unwilling sexual act. Kian Josiah was born on a Wednesday morning, January 21, 2004. I was nineteen years old then—a sophomore in college, senator of my class, a division II cheerleader, an RA (resident assistant), and oh yeah, a mother. I missed class Thursday and didn't have any Friday classes. School was closed due to a snowstorm for two more days so on January 28, I was back in class. I remember I had a science lab from 6:00 p.m. to 9:00 p.m. I walked down the hall and turned the corner. People who knew me went through the usual list of postpartum questions. Then there were a few people that made comments like, "She should have taken the semester off!" and "What happened to the baby?" They didn't know that my newborn was just a few buildings away with my mom. This lasted a few weeks, and then the next decision had to be made. My mom had left her job and husband for almost a month. It was time for her to go. There was no way that I could keep Kian with me on campus. I could stop being an RA, but that would mean I would owe my school $5,328. I could transfer to a school in Philadelphia, but I was a sophomore with junior status, and transferring would set me back two years. I could drop out of college, but if you think that, you really don't know me!

We drove from Richmond to Philadelphia, and at the end of that weekend my mom said to me, "I will keep him for you, but your GPA can't drop below a 3.0 or you will come home." With that I got on an Amtrak train and cried the two hundred and fifty miles back to Virginia. I made a calendar; I counted every fourteen days until I would see my son again.

With each day that I crossed off, I dealt with the ridicule of others; I was amazed that so many people would be that way. Then I came up with my slogan: if I finish school when he is two years old, I can take care of us for the rest of our lives. So I did it! I was awarded a child care scholarship by Family Care Solutions. Things started to look up for me.

Tiffany Jenkins-Stevens is a mother who was determined to stay involved in school activities after having her baby.

When Kian was still an infant, I was inducted into Kappa Delta Pi, an educational honor society. I came home for the summer and took classes at community college. I shocked everybody, even myself, when I became head RA, continued to cheer, and achieved one of my wildest dreams: I became a member of the Alpha Eta chapter of the Alpha Kappa Alpha Sorority Inc. in the spring of 2005. I felt like I had everything, but I wanted one more thing—to be Miss Virginia Union University. My grades, activities, and reputation on campus spoke for themselves. I went to the interest meeting, and on the last page of the application there it was: "Contestants may not be or have ever been pregnant or married." I thought I was defeated that day but not so. I wouldn't be the queen of my school, but I was the queen of my class. My son's godfather was the senior class king, therefore Kian rightfully earned the nickname "Baby Senior" on our campus.

> With each day that I crossed off, I dealt with the ridicule of others; I was amazed that so many people would be that way.

My count down to May 14, 2006, began. It was my mom's birthday and my graduation day. Everything and everybody else was a blur to me until they called my name. "Tiffany Jenkins, cum laude." I looked down at my apparel and counted the honors draped around my neck, and at that moment, I was overwhelmed with joy. For I didn't just graduate from college on time with a baby, but I graduated with honors! This evening, as I look around my house, I watch my son play, and I know how much he is loved. And, yes, God did heal my hurt and my pain, and my son no longer represents that circumstance in my life, but he became that force to push me through my college years.

Tiffany Jenkins-Stevens credits her success to the favor of God and the unfailing love of her parents. She graduated with honors from Virginia Union University in 2006 with a bachelor of science degree in exceptional education. Tiffany is a special education teacher at Boushall Middle School. She currently resides in Richmond, Virginia, with her husband, Robert Stevens II, and her son, Kian.

Meet Tammy

I cried for three days when I found out that I was pregnant! This is not how I planned it. I still had one year of full-time classes to take. How was I going to raise a baby and go to school, especially by myself? It was hard enough before I was having a baby.

On May 24, 2006, I became the proud mother of a beautiful baby boy. His father was not around; he had stopped speaking to us when I was about five months pregnant, and he wanted nothing to do with having a baby. When I held my son in my arms for the first time, my heart melted. My mother stayed with me for the first two weeks to help, even though I insisted on doing it by myself. The six weeks of maternity leave were some of the most wonderful times I had had in a long time. I was sleep deprived, but that didn't seem to matter. I enjoyed spending so much time with Isaac and all the cuddling. Those six weeks went by so smoothly but too quickly. Then I returned to work. This was hard after being home so much with Isaac. Being a single mom and living on my own, I needed money, so I worked two jobs. My mother watched Isaac for me for free, and I could not have done it without her.

In August Isaac was three months old, and it was time for me to start back to school. I went back as a full-time student working one job. My mother continued to watch Isaac for me. I would do homework after Isaac was in bed; I would almost always fall asleep typing at the computer. I would finally get my homework done around 2:00 a.m., and Isaac would be up at 3:00 a.m. to drink from a bottle. My alarm would go off around 6:00 a.m., and sometimes I would sit up and cry because I did not think I could do it anymore. I was so tired, physically and emotionally. I would only get to see Isaac for about two hours a day; my mom pretty much helped me raise him during this time. This was not easy for her either. I wanted to give up on many occasions, but I didn't. Isaac was my everyday reminder of why what I was doing was so important. We would both be better

Tammy Richardson is a mother who learned that too much was too much and gave up her two jobs.

off at the end. I made it through that semester but said I would never go to school as a full-time student again. I would rather be in school longer by going part time than to go full time and not make it through at all.

I got a chance to take some breathing time over Christmas break and was ready to go to school part time in January. At this point I was hardly working. By September I had quit my job to focus on my last semester of school. I used my income tax money to pay all my bills through September when school refunds would become available. I also received food stamps, medical assistance, and Section 8 housing assistance. I did not feel proud about getting help, but that is what these programs are there for. It was more important for me to take care of Isaac and finish school than to feel down about getting help.

> *I also received food stamps, medical assistance, and Section 8 housing assistance. I did not feel proud about getting help, but that is what these programs are there for.*

Family, friends, and my own dedication got me through this semester. I had one more semester to go.

This last semester was not easy. I had a practicum, another class, and a very active seventeen-month-old. My practicum meant three days a week of at least five hours of student teaching, a two-hour meeting every two weeks, and constructing a portfolio (and don't forget all the homework that goes with it). Then I had another class that required writing and implementing lesson plans. Then there was Isaac. He required so much of my time and energy that I had to go to bed when he did, or I didn't get any sleep. But I couldn't do homework with him awake. I spent many nights falling asleep while trying to do homework.

Many times I wanted to give up. I had a wonderful support system. However, the most important part of your support system is you. You need to believe that you can do it and remember that it is worth the sacrifices. If you do not believe in what you are doing

Professor, May I Bring My Baby to Class?

and that you can do it, then the other support does not matter. Sometimes you may need to swallow your pride and ask for help. Never stop believing in what you are fighting for: a better life for you and your child.

Tammy Richardson resides in Watsontown, Pennsylvania, with her son, Isaac. Tammy earned her associate degree in early childhood education from Pennsylvania College of Technology in December 2007. She enjoys reading and spending time with her son and taking long walks in the park.

Meet**Moneek**

The year 1997 marked two major accomplishments in my life: I completed my first year at Moore College of Art & Design, and I gave birth to my sons in August. One month after my children were born I went back to school part time. But juggling the care that two infants required and a part-time class load proved to be overwhelming, and despite all of my efforts and ambition, I did not pass that semester. I then decided to take off the spring and give my sons my full attention.

In September 1998 I went back to school full time with solid academic records. My sons attended a reputable child care center in Philadelphia. I was comfortable knowing that my children were happy and safe at the day care, and I appreciated the fact that they were in educational day care. Unfortunately, quality child care often comes with a steep price tag, and tuition for children in my sons' age group was $145 per week, per child.

I believe that every penny spent on child care for my sons has been money well spent, but at the time with my current financial situation, day care had quickly became a "luxury" that I would not be able to afford. I felt as though I was quickly running out of options. I had followed up every lead I had gotten for possible financial assistance for day care, to no avail. I did not qualify for

Moneek Pines-Elliott is a mother who used her college savings and loans to help pay the high cost of child care for her twin sons before finding financial support so she could finish school.

subsidies, and my sons were not yet old enough for Head Start. The local welfare department told me that I would have to stop going to college and work at least twenty-five hours a week to qualify for government subsidy. I called the mayor's office, I spoke with my state representative and met with the president of my college. Despite being an all women's school, my college did not provide a day care program, nor was there any type of assistance available—an issue I did not address while serving on the student government.

I refused to succumb to the stress of not knowing how I was going to pay for day care. I stayed focused and positive about my situation, and I held on to the faith that things would work out for the best. After all, my children's well-being is always my number-one priority.

I searched for a scholarship and was awarded one. It was a tremendous help. I will be forever grateful to Family Care Solutions for helping. I realized just how much both my sons love to learn. Even at their young ages, they seemed to hunger for knowledge, and the wonderful people at the day care helped me feed that hunger.

Like my sons, I too, hungered for knowledge and education. By educating myself, I helped ensure that my boys would be exposed to all that is possible and available in this world. My college degree has helped me achieve my goals, both for my children and myself.

Moneek Pines-Elliott lives in Philadelphia, Pennsylvania, with her husband and three sons. She is a 2001 graduate of Moore College of Art & Design. She recently opened a child care center that focuses on the arts and plans to give back by helping other young mothers in college with child care. She enjoys spending time with her family, shopping, and fashion.

CHAPTER 6

Reflections of Your College Years

Throughout this book you've been reading stories about mothers like you. Now it's your turn to tell your story in the pages of this book or share your story with others at our Web site, http://www.studentparentjournal.com.

The future belongs to those who believe in the beauty of their dreams.

Eleanor Roosevelt

_____

_____

_____

_____

_____

_____

_____

_____

_____

_____

_____

Professor, May I Bring My Baby to Class?

_____

_____

_____

_____

_____

_____

_____

_____

_____

_____

_____

_____

_____

_____

_____

_____

_____

_____

_____

_____

_____

Professor, May I Bring My Baby to Class?

Professor, May I Bring My Baby to Class?

Professor, May I Bring My Baby to Class?

Professor, May I Bring My Baby to Class?

CHAPTER 7

Graduation Day

Congratulations! You did it. After the hard work, late nights, and sacrifices, go ahead and be proud, smile, laugh, and enjoy this day. You deserve to be honored, recognized, singled out, and loved. Use this space to acknowledge your children and supporters. List your degrees and document your accomplishments. Use the blank pages that follow for good wishes from those who've helped you along this journey (family, friends, teachers, professors, counselors, and social workers, etc.).

All great achievements require time.

Maya Angelou

It's all about me

_____

(your name)

Education is something no one can take from you. Now pass that principle on to your children.

Glue a picture of your family here.

_____   _____

(your child's name)   *(your child's name)*

_____   _____

(your child's name)   *(your child's name)*

Schools I attended

School name	Graduation date	Degree/certificate

Here's what I am most proud of:

_____

_____

_____

_____

_____

_____

_____

_____

_____

_____

_____

Keeping it REAL

I am grateful to those who helped me achieve my goals.
(Write how they helped you through your college
years.)

Name

Message

_____ *for* _____

_____ *for* _____

_____ *for* _____

_____ *for* _____

_____ *for* _____

_____ *for* _____

_____ *for* _____

_____ *for* _____

_____ *for* _____

_____ *for* _____

Resources

SUPPORT ORGANIZATIONS

The following is a list of organizations and their Web sites to help you address your needs:

- ❱ National Network to End Violence (800-799-7233): http://www.nnedv.org

- ❱ National Domestic Violence Hotline (800-799-7233): http://www.ndvh.org

- ❱ Rape, Abuse & Incest National Network (800-656-HOPE): http://www.rainn.org

- ❱ National Alliance of Mental Illness (800-950-6264): http://www.nami.org

- ❱ Depression & Bipolar Support Alliance (800-826-3632): http://www.dbsalliance.org

- ❱ National Coalition for the Homeless (202-462-4822): http://www.nationalhomeless.org

- ❱ Corporation for Supportive Housing: http://www.csh.org

- ❱ AIDS Alliance for Children, Youth, and Families (202-785-3564): http://www.aids-alliance.org

- ❱ Jim Casey Youth Opportunities Initiative for those aging out of foster care (314-863-7000): http://www.jimcaseyyouth.org

- ❱ National Women's Law Center (202-588-5180): http://www.nwlc.org

CAREER OPPORTUNITIES

The following is a list of Web sites that allow you to explore career opportunities (some include career videos):

- Peterson's: http://www.petersons.com
- College Board: http://www.collegeboard.com
- Career Voyages: http://www.careervoyages.gov
- Going2College: http://www.going2college.org
- Mapping Your Future: http://www.mappingyourfuture.org
- Education Planner: http://www.educationplanner.com

POSTSECONDARY INSTITUTION ACCREDITING AGENCIES

The following is a list of agencies and their Web sites to help you learn more about accrediting postsecondary institutions, accrediting agencies, fake degrees, and scholarship scams:

- U.S. Department of Education, Office of Postsecondary Education: http://www.ope.ed.gov/accreditation/
- Council for Higher Education Accreditation: http://www.chea.org
- World Wide Learn: http://www.worldwidelearn.com/accreditation
- Federal Trade Commission: http://www.ftc.gov

CAMPUS CHILD CARE CENTERS

The following is a list of organizations to help you identify on-campus child care centers at colleges and universities:

- National Center for Education Statistics: http://www.nces.ed.gov
- National Coalition for Campus Children's Centers: http://www.campuschildren.org

COLLEGE PREPARATION

The following is a list of organizations and their Web sites to help you learn about and prepare for the SAT and ACT tests, learn more about the Student Aid Report (SAR), and find tips on applying to college:

- College Board: http://www.collegeboard.com
- ACT: http://www.act.org
- Education Planner: http://www.educationplanner.org
- Federal Student Aid: http://www.studentaid.ed.gov

RETURNING TO SCHOOL

The following is a list of community college support programs and their Web sites:

- Gateway to College: http://www.gatewaytocollege.org
- Achieving the Dream: http://www.achievingthedream.org

COLLEGE LOANS

The following is a list of organizations and their Web sites to help you learn more about the types of loans that are available:

- American Education Services: http://www.aessuccess.org
- College Board: http://www.collegeboard.com
- Financial Aid: http://www.finaid.org
- Federal Student Aid: http://www.studentaid.ed.gov
- U.S. Department of Education: http://www.ed.gov

FEDERAL STUDENT AID FOR COLLEGE

The following is the Web site where you can find the federal student aid application and state deadlines:

- Free Application for Federal Student Aid (FAFSA): http://www.fafsa.ed.gov

OTHER TYPES OF STUDENT AID FOR COLLEGE

The following is a list of organizations and their Web sites offering scholarships and grants to students, women, single mothers, and student-parents:

- American Association of Colleges of Nursing: http://www.aacn.nche.edu
- American Association of University Women Educational Foundation: http://www.aauw.org
- American Indian College Fund: http://www.collegefund.org
- Association for Women in Sciences: http://www.awis.org
- Chafee Education and Training Vouchers for foster youth: http://www.statevoucher.org

- Education Foundation for Women in Accounting: http://www.efwa.org
- Education Planner: http://www.educationplanner.com
- Executive Women International: http://www.executivewomen.org
- Fast Web Scholarship Search: http://www.fastweb.com
- Hispanic College Fund: http://www.hispanicfund.org
- Hispanic Scholarship Fund: http://www.hsf.net
- Jack Kent Cooke Foundation: http://www.jkcf.org
- Jeannette Rankin Foundation: http://www.rankinfoundation.org
- Orphan Foundation of America Scholarships: http://www.orphan.org
- Patsy Takemoto Mink Education Foundation: http://www.patsyminkfoundation.org
- Presidential Freedom Scholarship: http://www.nationalservice.org
- Society of Women Engineers: http://www.swe.org
- Talbots Women's Scholarship Fund: http://www.thetalbotsinc.com/brands/talbots/charitable.asp
- The Congressional Hispanic Caucus Institute: http://www.chciyouth.org
- The Jackie Robinson Foundation: http://www.jackierobinson.org
- The Gates Millennium Scholars: http://www.gmsp.org
- The R.O.S.E. Fund: http://www.rosefund.org
- Tom Joyner Foundation: http://www.blackamericaweb.com/?q=tjf_tjfoundation
- United Negro College Fund: http://www.uncf.org
- Women's Opportunity Grant: http://www.soroptimist.org
- Women's Sports Foundation: http://www.womensportsfoundation.org

ACCREDITING CHILD CARE ORGANIZATIONS

The following is a list of organizations and their Web sites listing accredited early child care programs:

- National Association of the Education of Young Children: http://www.naeyc.org
- National Association of Family Child Care: http://www.nafcc.org

- National Early Childhood Program Accreditation:
  http://www.necpa.net
- National Association of Child Care Professionals:
  http://www.naccp.org

CHOOSING QUALITY CHILD CARE

The following is a list of organizations and their Web sites to help you find quality child care, learn more about choosing quality child care programs, and learn about quality rating systems:

- Child Care Aware: http://www.childcareaware.org
- U.S. Department of Health and Human Services, Administration of Children and Families: http://www.acf.hhs.gov/programs/ccb
- The National Child Care Information Center:
  http://www.nccic.org/topics/topic/index.cfm?topicId=5

EARLY LEARNING

The following is a list of organizations and their Web sites to help you learn more about the importance of choosing quality care and early learning:

- United Way Success By 6: http://national.unitedway.org/sb6
- Born Learning: http://www.bornlearning.org
- Think Big Start Small: http://www.thinkbigstartsmall.org
- PBS Parents: http://www.pbs.org/parents/earlylearning

STUDENT AID FOR CHILD CARE

The following is a list of national organizations and their Web sites where you can find help to pay for child care:

- YMCA: http://www.ymca.net
- Boys and Girls Club: http://www.bgca.org
- Child Care Aware (to find your local resource and referral agency):
  http://www.childcareaware.org
- Child Care Access Means Parents In School (CCAMPIS):
  http://www.ed.gov/programs/campisp
- Head Start: http://www.acf.hhs.gov/programs/ohs

STUDENT-PARENT SUPPORT PROGRAMS

The following colleges and universities offer student-parent support programs:

School	On-campus child care center?	On-campus housing for single parents and children?	Grants, scholarships, stipends for student-parents?	Dedicated office supporting student-parent issues?	Student-parent support group on campus?
Alverno College http://www.alverno.edu Milwaukee, Wisconsin	yes	yes	child care	no	no
Baldwin-Wallace College http://www.bw.edu Berea, Ohio	yes	yes	books, transportation	Single Parents Reaching Out for Unassisted Tomorrows (SPROUT)	no
Carteret Community College http://www.carteret.edu Morehead City, North Carolina	no	no	child care, books, transportation	no	yes
Community College of Philadelphia http://www.ccp.edu Philadelphia, Pennsylvania	yes	no	child care	Women's Center	no
Clovis Community College http://www.clovis.edu Clovis, New Mexico	yes	no	child care, books, transportation, living expenses	student services	no
College of St. Mary http://www.csm.edu Omaha, Nebraska	yes	yes	child care, books, meal plan for children, living expenses	Office of Student Development—Mothers Living and Learning	no
Cornell University http://www.ohr.cornell .edu/worklife Ithaca, New York	yes	yes	child care	no	yes
Danville Community College http://www.dcc.vccs.edu Danville, Virginia	yes	no	child care	student services	yes

School	On-campus child care center?	On-campus housing for single parents and children?	Grants, scholarships, stipends for student-parents?	Dedicated office supporting student-parent issues?	Student-parent support group on campus?
Eastfield College http://www .eastfieldcollege.com Mesquite, Texas	yes	no	child care, meal plan for children	no	no
Eastern Kentucky University http://www.eku.edu Richmond, Kentucky	yes	yes	books, tuition	Education Plays Center	yes
East Tennessee State University http://www.etsu.edu Johnson City, Tennessee	yes	no	child care	no	no
El Paso Community College http://www.epcc.edu El Paso, Texas	yes	no	child care, books, off-campus housing for parent/children, living expenses	no	yes
Endicott College http://www.endicott.edu Beverly, Massachusetts	no	yes	child care, meal plan for children	Keys to Degrees Program	yes
Humboldt State University http://www.humboldt.edu Arcata, California	yes	yes	child care, books, meal plan for children, off-campus housing for parent/children, living expenses	no	no
Illinois Valley Community College http://www.ivcc.edu Oglesby, Illinois	yes	no	child care, books, meal plan for children	Early Childhood Center Office	no
Inter American University of Puerto Rico http://www.inter.edu	yes	no	child care	no	yes

School	On-campus child care center?	On-campus housing for single parents and children?	Grants, scholarships, stipends for student-parents?	Dedicated office supporting student-parent issues?	Student-parent support group on campus?
Jefferson College http://www.jeffco.edu Hillsboro, Missouri	yes	no	child care, books, meal plan for children, off-campus housing for parent/children, living expenses	no	yes
Linn-Benton Community College http://www.linnbenton .edu Albany, Oregon	yes	no	child care	Family Connections	yes
Los Medanos College http://www.losmedanos .edu Pittsburg, California	yes	no	child care, books	no	no
Manor College http://www.manor.edu Jenkintown, Pennsylvania	no	no	child care	no	no
Metropolitan Community College http://www.mccneb.edu Omaha, Nebraska	no	no	child care, books, transportation	student services	yes
Minnesota Office of Higher Education* http://www.ohe.state .mn.us St. Paul, Minnesota	contact school of choice	yes	contact school of choice	Postsecondary Child Care Grant Program Administration	no
Misericordia University http://www.misericordia .edu Dallas, Pennsylvania	no	yes	child care, books, meal plan for children, off-campus housing for parent/ children, living expenses, tuition	Women with Children Program	yes
Missouri State University http://www.missouristate .edu/ Springfield, Missouri	yes	yes	child care, meal plan for children	adult student services	no

School	On-campus child care center?	On-campus housing for single parents and children?	Grants, scholarships, stipends for student-parents?	Dedicated office supporting student-parent issues?	Student-parent support group on campus?
Monroe Community College http://www.monroecc.edu Rochester, New York	yes	no	child care	student services	no
Peralta Community College District http://www.peralta.edu Oakland, California	yes	no	child care, meal plan for children	Children's Center	yes
Pennsylvania College of Technology http://www.pct.edu Williamsport, Pennsylvania	yes	no	child care, meal plan for children	no	no
Penn State University http://www.psu.edu University Park, Pennsylvania	yes	yes	child care	no	no
St. Paul's College http://www.saintpauls.edu Lawrenceville, Virginia	yes	yes	child care, living expenses	Single Parent Support System (SPSS)	yes
Texas College http://www.texascollegeon-line.net Tyler, Texas	yes	no	child care, books, transportation	Single Parent Suppor Services	yes
The Ohio State University http://www.osu.edu Columbus, Ohio	yes	yes	child care, books, housing, living expenses	ACCESS Collaborative Office of Minority Affairs	yes
University of Colorado at Colorado Springs http://www.uccs.edu Colorado Springs, Colorado	yes	no	child care	no	
University of Massachusetts Amherst http://www.umass.edu Amherst, Massachusetts	yes	yes	child care	Office of Family Resources	no

School	On-campus child care center?	On-campus housing for single parents and children?	Grants, scholarships, stipends for student-parents?	Dedicated office supporting student-parent issues?	Student-parent support group on campus?
University of Missouri–St. Louis http://www.umsl.edu St. Louis, Missouri	yes	no	child care	Office of Student Affairs	no
University of New England http://www.une.edu Biddeford, Maine	no	no	books, matched savings account		yes
University of Wisconsin–Milwaukee http://www4.uwm.edu Milwaukee, Wisconsin	yes	no	child care, books, transportation, off-campus housing, living expenses, tuition	Life Impact Program	yes
Utah Valley University http://www.uvu.edu Orem, Utah	yes	no	child care, books, meal plan for children	Women's Resource Center and Turning Point	yes
Washington State Community College http://www.wscc.edu Marietta, Ohio	yes	no	child care	no	no
West Virginia University http://www.wvu.edu Morgantown, West Virginia	yes	no	child care	Child Development & Family Support Services	yes
Wilson College http://www.wilson.edu Chambersburg, Pennyslvania	yes	yes	child care, books, living expenses, meal plans for children	Women with Children Program	no
Winston-Salem State University http://www.wssu.edu Winston-Salem, North Carolina	yes	no		Office of Student Advocacy & Services for Adult and Graduate Students	

* State funds are allocated via this office to eligible postsecondary institutions in Minnesota to help students pursuing a postsecondary education pay for child care.

Is This the Right Place for My Child?

38 RESEARCH-BASED INDICATORS OF HIGH-QUALITY CHILD CARE

This table was developed by the National Association of Child Care Resource and Referral Agencies to be used as a checklist to help you identify and measure quality child care. Make a photocopy of this checklist for each child care facility you visit and ask these questions. Your answers will help you compare child care programs and choose which program is best for you and your child. For more information about this checklist visit http://www.naccrra.org/for_parents/quality_indicators.php.

Is This the Right Place for My Child?

(Make a copy of this checklist to use with each program you visit.)

naccrra
National Association of Child Care
Resource & Referral Agencies

Place a check in the box if the program meets your expectations.

Will my child be supervised?

	Are children watched at all times, including when they are sleeping?[15]
	Are adults warm and welcoming? Do they pay individual attention to each child?[40]
	Are positive guidance techniques used? Do adults avoid yelling, spanking, and other negative punishments?[16]
	Are the caregiver/teacher-to-child ratios appropriate and do they follow the recommended guidelines: ▶ One caregiver per 3 or 4 infants ▶ One caregiver per 3 or 4 young toddlers ▶ One caregiver per 4 to 6 older toddlers ▶ One caregiver per 6 to 9 preschoolers[19]

Have the adults been trained to care for children?

	If a center: ▶ Does the director have a degree and some experience in caring for children?[27/28/29] ▶ Do the teachers have a credential*** or Associate's degree and experience in caring for children?[27/28/29] **If a family child care home:** ▶ Has the provider had specific training on children's development and experience caring for children?[30]
	Is there always someone present who has current CPR and first aid training?[32]
	Are the adults continuing to receive training on caring for children?[33]
	Have the adults been trained on child abuse prevention and how to report suspected cases?[12/13]

Will my child be able to grow and learn?

	For older children, are there specific areas for different kinds of play (books, blocks, puzzles, art, etc.)?[21]
	For infants and toddlers, are there toys that "do something" when the child plays with them?[41]
	Is the play space organized and are materials easy-to-use? Are some materials available at all times?[21]
	Are there daily or weekly activity plans available? Have the adults planned experiences for the children to enjoy? Will the activities help children learn?[22]
	Do the adults talk with the children during the day? Do they engage them in conversations? Ask questions, when appropriate?[43]
	Do the adults read to children at least twice a day or encourage them to read, if they can read?[43]

Is this a safe and healthy place for my child?

	Do adults and children wash their hands (before eating or handling food, or after using the bathroom, changing diapers, touching body fluids or eating, etc.)?[4]
	Are diaper changing surfaces cleaned and sanitized after each use?[5]
	Do all of the children enrolled have the required immunizations?[6]
	Are medicines labeled and out of children's reach?[7]
	Are adults trained to give medicines and keep records of medications?[7]
	Are surfaces used to serve food cleaned and sanitized?
	Are the food and beverages served to children nutritious, and are they stored, prepared, and served in the right way to keep children growing and healthy?
	Are cleaning supplies and other poisonous materials locked up, out of children's reach?[8]
	Is there a plan to follow if a child is injured, sick or lost?[9]

Notes:

_____
_____
_____
_____
_____
_____
_____
_____
_____
_____
_____
_____
_____
_____
_____
_____
_____
_____
_____
_____
_____
_____
_____
_____
_____
_____
_____
_____
_____
_____
_____
_____
_____
_____
_____
_____

Is This the Right Place for My Child? 38 Research-Based Indicators of High-Quality Child-Care

Appendix B

	Place a check in the box if the program meets your expectations.
	Are first aid kits readily available?[10]
	Is there a plan for responding to disasters (fire, flood, etc.)?[11]
	Has a satisfactory criminal history background check been conducted on each adult present? ▶ Was the check based on fingerprints?[14]
	Have all the adults who are left alone with children had background and criminal screenings?[13] **In a center:** ▶ Are two adults with each group of children most of the time? **In a home:** ▶ Are family members left alone with children only in emergencies?
	Is the outdoor play area a safe place for children to play?[39] ▶ Is it checked each morning for hazards before children use it?[23] ▶ Is the equipment the right size and type for the age of the children who use it?[24] ▶ In center-based programs, is the playground area surrounded by a fence at least 4 feet tall?[25] ▶ Is the equipment placed on mulch, sand, or rubber matting?[23] ▶ Is the equipment in good condition?[39]
	Is the number of children in each group limited? ▶ In family child care homes and centers, children are in groups of no more than** ■ 6-8 infants ■ 6-12 younger toddlers ■ 8-12 older toddlers ■ 12-20 preschoolers ■ 20-24 school-agers[20]

	Is the program set up to promote quality?
	Does the program have the highest level of licensing offered by the state?[42]
	Are there written personnel policies and job descriptions?[17]
	Are parents and staff asked to evaluate the program?[37]
	Are staff evaluated each year; do providers do a self-assessment?[18]
	Is there a written annual training plan for staff professional development?[33]
	Is the program evaluated each year by someone outside the program?[38]
	Is the program accredited by a national organization?[36]

	Does the program work with parents?
	Will I be welcome any time my child is in care?[1]
	Is parents' feedback sought and used in making program improvements?[1]
	Will I be given a copy of the program's policies?[2]
	Are annual conferences held with parents?[3]

These questions are based on research about child care; you can read the research findings on the NACCRRA website under "Questions for Parents to Ask" at http://www.naccrra.org. Research-based indicators can only describe quality. Parents should base their decisions on actual observations.

* These are the adult-to-child ratios and group sizes recommended by the National Association for the Education of Young Children. Ratios are lowered when there are one or more children who may need additional help to fully participate in a program due to a disability, or other factors.

** Group sizes are considered the maximum number of children to be in a group, regardless of the number of adult staff.

*** Individuals working in child care can earn a Child Development Associate credential.

For help finding child care in your area, contact Child Care Aware, a Program of NACCRRA at 1-800-424-2246 or www.childcareaware.org.

For information about other AAP publications visit: www.aap.org

Endorsed by:

American Academy of Pediatrics
DEDICATED TO THE HEALTH OF ALL CHILDREN™

Is This the Right Place for My Child? 38 Research-Based Indicators of High-Quality Child Care

NOTES

Managing My Schedule

Create a monthly calendar to share with your support team so each member is aware of your late nights, test dates, and after-school appointments. Use the calendar to assign responsibilities to your team members. See the example on page 169 of how to create your team calendar. Use the blank calendar on page 170 to create your own team calendar. You may also make copies of the blank calendar or print from our Web site at http://www.studentparentjournal.com.

Your schedule may include the following types of activities (but are certainly not limited to):

- ▶ Doctor's appointments—yours or your child's

- ▶ Child care schedule—who's picking your child up when you have to study late

- ▶ Work schedule—so everyone will know when you're at work

- ▶ Appointments

- ▶ Study-group sessions

- ▶ Finals

List your support team members here. Share this list with everyone on your team. Make copies of this page as necessary, or print more from http://www.studentparentjournal.com. Remember, your team may change each semester or quarter.

School _____ Semester/Quarter _____ Year _____

Support-team member _____

Availability _____

Phone number/ e-mail _____

School _____ Semester/Quarter _____ Year _____

Support-team member _____

Availability _____

Phone number/ e-mail _____

School _____ Semester/Quarter _____ Year _____

Support-team member _____

Availability _____

Phone number/ e-mail _____

School _____ Semester/Quarter _____ Year _____

Support-team member _____

Availability _____

Phone number/ e-mail _____

Month __December__ Year __2009__

Responsible Team Member	MONDAY	TUESDAY	WEDNESDAY	THURSDAY	FRIDAY	SATURDAY	SUNDAY
Grandmom		1	2	3	4	5 *Group Project, library from 1 p.m. to 4 p.m.*	6
David	7	8	9 *Shawn's class trip @ day care*	10	11	12	13
Aunt Sarah & Uncle Joe	14	15	16	17 *Shawn's doctor appt. @ 1 p.m.*	18	19	20
David	21 FINALS *Pick up Shawn/ late night at library*	22 *Pick up Shawn/ late night at library*	23 FINALS	24	25	26 *Group Study 9 a.m.–1 p.m.*	27
Grandmom	28	29	30	31			

Year ___

Month ___

Responsible Team Member	MONDAY	TUESDAY	WEDNESDAY	THURSDAY	FRIDAY	SATURDAY	SUNDAY

Appendix C

Notes

CHAPTER 1

1. Salary.com, Personal Salary Wizard, http://www.salary.com (accessed December 7, 2008).

2. U.S. Census Bureau, Current Population Survey (CPS), Annual Social and Economic (ASEC) Supplement, PINC-04 Educational Attainment-People 18 Years Old and Over, by Total Money Earnings in 2007, Work Experience in 2007, Age, Pace, Hispanic Origin, and Sex, http://pubdb3.census.gov/macro/032008/perinc/new04_000.htm (accessed February 9, 2009).

3. Sheryl Gay Stolberg, *"Obama Signs Equal-Pay Legislation,"* The New York Times, January 29, 2009, http://www.nytimes.com/2009/01/30/us/politics/30ledbetter-web.html?hp (accessed January 29, 2009).

CHAPTER 2

1. U.S. Department of Education Institute of Education Sciences, National Center for Statistics Education, Integrated Postsecondary Education Data Systems (IPEDS) Survey, http://nces.ed.gov/surveys/ (accessed August 25, 2008).

2. College Board, "Types of Colleges," http://www.collegeboard.com/student/csearch/where-to-start/2.html (accessed December 12, 2006).

3. U.S. Department of Education, "Archived: Preparing Your Child for College—General Questions about College," http://www.ed.gov/pubs/Prepare/pt1.html (accessed December 12, 2006).

4. Philadelphia Workforce Investment Board, "A Tale of Two Cities Fact Sheet," 2007, http://pwib.org/downloads/TaleofTwoCities.pdf.

5. Ibid.

6. Ibid.

7. Ibid.

8. Ibid.

9. American Association for Community Colleges, "Community College Fast Facts," http://www2.aacc.nche.edu/research/home.htm (accessed August 22, 2008).

10. Council for Higher Education Accreditation, "Degree Mills and Accreditation Mills: Important Questions about Accreditation," http://www.chea.org/degreemills/default.htm (accessed December 7, 2008).

11. World Wide Learn, "Why You Should Choose an Accredited College Degree," http://www .worldwidelearn.com/accreditation/importance-accreditation.htm (accessed November 13, 2008).

12. Ibid; U.S. Department of Education, "Prepare for My Future: Diploma Mills and Accreditation-Diploma Mills," http://www.ed.gov/students/prep/college/diplomamills/diploma-mills.html (accessed December 7, 2008).

13. Ibid.

14. Wilson Marketing Group, http://www.wmg-earlychildhood.com/ecmarket.php.

15. Federal Trade Commission, Protecting America's Consumers, "Scholarship Scams," http://www.ftc .gov/bcp/edu/microsites/scholarship/index.shtml (accessed December 7, 2008).

16. American Association of Community Colleges, "Community College Fast Facts," http://www2.aacc .nche.edu/research/home.htm (accessed August 22, 2008).

17. Gateway to College, "The Gateway to College Program," http://www.gatewaytocollege.org (accessed February 6, 2008).

18. Ibid.

19. Achieving the Dream, "What Is Achieving the Dream?" http://www.achievingthedream.org (accessed February 6, 2008).

20. The Kalamazoo Promise, https://www.kalamazoopromise.com/?mode.page.view=76 (accessed December 7, 2008).

21. FAFSA: Free Application for Federal Student Aid, "Federal Student Aid FAFSA," http://www.fafsa .ed.gov/.

22. American Education Services, "Education Planner," http://www.educationplanner.com/ education_planner/paying_article.asp?sponsor=2859&articleName=Filling_Out_the_FAFSA (accessed December 8, 2008).

23. Felicia Kitzmiller, "College Bound: Financial Aid Help for First-Generation College Students," independentmail.com, August 12, 2007, http://www.independentmail.com/news/2007/aug/12/ college-bound-financial-aid-help-first-generation-/ (accessed August 13, 2007).

24. Pennsylvania Higher Education Assistance Agency, "The 5 Steps to Financial Aid," http:// www.pheaa.org/plan_for_college/5Steps/index.shtml?s=H26 (accessed December 8, 2008).

25. Free Application for Federal Student Aid, "Before Beginning a FAFSA," http://fafsa.ed.gov/ before001.htm (accessed December 8, 2008).

26. College Financial Aid Guide, "Federal Grants for College Students," http://www.collegefinancialaidguide.com/student/federal-grants-college-students.html (accessed January 2, 2007).

27. Barbara Lauren, "Yale and Harvard Financial Aid Plans Put Pressure on Less Wealthy Colleges," American Association of Collegiate Registrars and Admission Officers, January 16, 2008, also available on-line at http://www.aacrao.org/transcript/index.cfm?fuseaction=show_view&doc_id=3754; Mary Beth Marklein, "Yale Becomes Latest to Boost Financial Aid," *USA Today*, January 16, 2008, http://www.usatoday.com/news/education/2008-01-14-yale-cost_N.htm (accessed August 22, 2008).

28. College Financial Aid Guide, "Federal Grants for College Students," http://www .collegefinancialaidguide.com/student/federal-grants-college-students.html (accessed January 22, 2007).

29. Community College of Philadelphia, "Dual Admissions Programs," http://www.ccp.edu/site/ prospective/dual_admissions/chartinfo.php (accessed December 8, 2008).

30. SuperPages.com, "What Are Different Types of Colleges and Universities?" http://www.superpages. com/supertips/types-of-colleges-and-universities.html (accessed December 12, 2006).

31. Maria Estarellas, "What You Should Know About Scholarships," College Financial Aid Guide, http://www.collegefinancialaidguide.com/scholarships/scholarships-know.htm (accessed January 22, 2007).

32. Jim Turner, "Parents, College-Bound Students Warned about Financial Aid Scams," TCPalm.com, August 2, 2007, http://www.tcpalm.com/news/2007/aug/02/parents-college-bound-students -warned-about-financ/ (accessed December 8, 2008).

CHAPTER 3

1. National Association of Child Care Resource & Referral Agencies, "Quality Child Care Makes a Difference," http://www.naccrra.org/policy/background_issues/quality_matters.php (accessed December 8, 2008).

2. Child Care Aware, "Types of Care," http://www.childcareaware.org/en/child_care_101/types_of _care/ (accessed December 8, 2008).

3. Child Care Aware, "Accreditation," http://www.childcareaware.org/en/parent_information/ accreditation.php (accessed December 8, 2008); U.S. Department of Health and Family Services, Administration for Children & Families, National Child Care Information and Technical Assistance Center, "Quality Rating Systems: Definition and Statewide Systems," http://nccic.acf.hhs.gov/ pubs/qrs-defsystems.html (accessed November 19, 2008).

4. U.S. Department of Health and Family Services, Administration for Children & Families, National Child Care Information and Technical Assistance Center, "Quality Rating Systems: Definition and Statewide Systems," http://nccic.acf.hhs.gov/pubs/qrs-defsystems.html (accessed November 19, 2008).

5. Ibid.

6. National Association of Child Care Resource & Referral Agencies, "Is This the Right Place for My Child? 38 Research-Based Indicators of High-Quality Child Care," May 2008, http://www.naccrra. org/for_parents/quality_indicators.php.

7. Ibid.

8. American Association of American Colleges, "Community College Fast Facts," http://www2.aacc .nche.edu/research/home.htm (accessed August 22, 2008).

9. National Association of Child Care Resource & Referral Agencies, "Parents and the High Price of Child Care," 2008 Update, http://www.naccrra.org/docs/reports/price_report/Price_Report_2008_execsumm.pdf (accessed December 9, 2008).

10. Elizabeth Lower-Basch, "Education and Training for TANF Recipients," Center for Law and Social Policy, March 18, 2008, also available on-line at http://www.clasp.org/publications/ed_and_training_rules_for_tanf_2008.pdf; Gene Falk, The Temporary Assistance for Needy Families (TANF) Block Grant: A Primer on TANF Financing and Federal Requirements, Congressional Research Service Report for Congress, January 8, 2007, also available on-line at https://www.policyarchive.org/bitstream/handle/10207/2326/RL32748_20070108.pdf?sequence=1.

11. Department of Health and Human Services Administration for Children and Families office of Family Assistance, Helping Families Achieve Self-Sufficiency: A Guide on Funding Services for Children and Families through the TANF Program, http://www.acf.hhs.gov/programs/ofa/resources/funds2.pdf; Commonwealth of Pennsylvania Department of Public Welfare, "Keystone Education Yields Success: KEYS Program Guidelines," (Harrisburg, Pennsylvania, April 24, 2007).

12. Ibid.

13. U.S. Department of Health & Human Services, Administration for Children & Families, Office of Head Start, "About Head Start," http://eclkc.ohs.acf.hhs.gov/hslc/About%20Head%20Start (accessed December 9, 2008).

14. U.S. Department of Education, "Child Care Access Means Parents In School," http://www.ed.gov/programs/campisp/index.html (accessed December 9, 2008).

15. Child Care Aware, http://www.childcareaware.org/en/ (accessed December 9, 2008).

CHAPTER 4

1. PBS Parents, "Early Learning: Focus on Birth to Five—Tips for Raising Your Baby and Preschooler," http://www.pbs.org/parents/earlylearning/milestones.html (accessed December 9, 2008).

2. Teresa A. Morgan, "Benefits of Reading for Children—How Reading Can Help Concentration," Ezine Articles, http://ezinearticles.com/?Benefits-of-Reading-For-Children—How-Reading-Can-Help-Concentration&id=1679587 (accessed December 9, 2008).

CHAPTER 5

1. L. Horn and S. Nevill, "Profile of Undergraduates in U.S. Postsecondary Education Institutions: 2003-04 with a Special Analysis of Community College Students (NCES-184)," U.S. Department of Education (Washington D.C. National Center for Education Statistics, 2006), http://nces.ed.gov/pubsearch/pubsinfo.asp?pubid=2006184 (accessed January 5, 2008).

Index

About the Author

Sherrill W. Mosee is founder and president of Family Care Solutions, Inc. (FCS), a nonprofit organization located in Philadelphia, Pennsylvania. She is creator of the FCS Child Care Scholarship and the Yes Mommy Can teen parent program and is the founding member of the Greater Philadelphia Consortium to Provide Child Care Access to Student-Parents.

After graduating from the University of Maryland with a degree in electrical engineering, Mosee moved to Philadelphia, Pennsylvania, in 1986 to work as a test engineer. She later returned to school in pursuit of a master's degree. She earned her master's degree in electrical engineering in June 1991 from Drexel University. She completed her coursework on a Friday and went into labor on the following Monday to deliver her first child. Becoming a first-time mother opened Mosee's eyes to a whole new world. She no longer focused on writing software for test equipment but rather studied literature to decide which baby formula was best. As she prepared to return to work, finding a quality, affordable, nurturing, and safe child care provider became one of her most challenging experiences. Inadequate resources available in the Philadelphia region prompted Mosee to compose and publish the first of four editions of *Who's Who in Child Care (WWICC)*, a resource guide to help working parents find child care.

When Mosee's stepdaughter had a baby during her first year of college, she realized that many single mothers do not have the resources and support to allow them to remain in school and pay for child care. Mosee partnered with child care providers listed in *WWICC* and established the FCS Child Care Scholarship in 1998 to help low-income single mothers pay for child care while pursuing their dreams of earning college degrees.

Mosee is an advocate for low-income student-parents by helping them access child care while they pursue their higher educational goals. Her persistence in these matters led to the creation of a Philadelphia-based consortium of colleges and universities that uses federal funding to help student-parents (women and men) pay for child care.

Sherrill W. Mosee is wife to George and mother to Darius and Asia. They live in Philadelphia, Pennsylvania.

To book a speaking engagement or to order more books for your school, agency, or organization, please contact us at 877-264-9915 or visit http://www.fcsbooks.com.

We'd love to hear from you! ∾